Georgia Amson-Bradshaw

WAYLAND
www.waylandbooks.co.uk

First published in Great Britain in 2018 by Wayland

Copyright © Hodder and Stoughton Limited, 2018

Produced for Wayland by
White-Thomson Publishing Ltd
www.wtpub.co.uk

Series Editor: Georgia Amson-Bradshaw
Series Designer: Rocket Design (East Anglia) Ltd

ISBN: 978 1 5263 0648 7
10 9 8 7 6 5 4 3 2 1

Wayland
An imprint of
Hachette Children's Group
Part of Hodder & Stoughton
Carmelite House
50 Victoria Embankment
London EC4Y 0DZ

An Hachette UK Company
www.hachette.co.uk
www.hachettechildrens.co.uk

Printed in China

Picture acknowledgements:
Images from Shutterstock.com: Hannamariah 6c, Anastasia Mazeina 7bl, AlenaLitvin 9t,
Vladimir Sazonov 12br, NotionPic 13t, SavAleKon14b, John Gomez 15t, topseller 15b, Doremi 16,
Jaroslav Moravcik 17t, Ignat Zaytsev 17bl, Olha Solodenko 17br, dzenphoto 20t, zaxenart 20b,
photomaster 21t, GraphicsRF 24t, LiuSol 25b, violetblue 26t, Piotr Wawrzyniuk 26b, Alena Kaz 27b.
Images from wiki commons: Daniel Ramirez 6b, Zoë Helene Kindermann 21b

All illustrations on pages 12, 13, 18, 19, 22, 23 by Steve Evans

All design elements from Shutterstock.

Glossary words are shown in bold.

CONTENTS

CHANGING SEASONS

Spring, summer, autumn and winter are all seasons.

FOUR SEASONS

Lots of countries around the world have four seasons. Each season brings different weather, and the length of the day changes.

spring

summer

autumn

winter

WET AND DRY

Some countries, near the middle of the Earth, stay warm all year round. They have just two seasons: a rainy season and a dry season.

rainy

dry

REASON FOR THE SEASONS

The Earth is a big ball that moves around the Sun in space. It takes the Earth one year to circle around the Sun. At certain times of year, different parts of the Earth are closer to the Sun. This is what causes the four seasons.

The top half of the Earth is called the **Northern Hemisphere.**

The bottom half of the Earth is called the **Southern Hemisphere.**

SUMMER HERE, WINTER THERE

The seasons don't happen at the same time all over the world. When it is summer in the Northern Hemisphere, it is winter in the Southern Hemisphere. When it is winter in the Northern Hemisphere, it is summer in the Southern Hemisphere.

SPRING

In spring, the days get longer and the weather gets warmer.

SPRING TO LIFE

After the cold, dark winter, nature starts to come to life again in the spring. The temperature begins to rise and there is more daylight.

LONGER DAYS

During spring, the days get longer and the nights get shorter. For one day in spring, night and day are exactly the same length. We call this the **equinox**. It happens in March in the Northern Hemisphere, and September in the Southern Hemisphere.

← – – – 12 HOURS – – – →

APRIL SHOWERS

The weather in spring can change a lot. Some days are warm and sunny, but the weather can quickly become cold and windy. Spring often brings rain showers.

WOW!

Spring gets its name from 'springing time', which was the old name for the season. It is the time when new plants 'spring' from the earth.

BOING!

HIDE AND SEEK

When the weather is rainy and sunny at the same time, it can create a very special effect. Do you know what it is? Can you spot one hiding? Answer on page 28.

MAKE A RAIN GAUGE

Measure how much rain falls each day in spring with a homemade rain gauge. You'll need:

A permanent marker pen

Some scissors

A two-litre plastic bottle

A ruler

STEP ONE

Cut off the tapered top part of the bottle. This can be tricky, so ask an adult to do this part. Place the cut-off part upside down, inside the main body of the bottle.

Using the ruler and the permanent marker pen, mark a scale up the side of the bottle in centimetres, starting at the bottom.

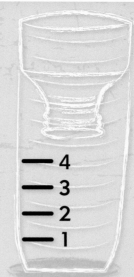

Take your rain gauge outside. Ensure it won't blow over by burying the bottom part a few centimetres into the ground.

After it has rained, check to see how far up the scale the water has risen. Empty out the water and replace your rain gauge, ready to begin recording again. Keep a record of how many centimetres of rain fall each day.

Date	Rainfall
7 May	0.5 cm
8 May	2 cm
9 May	0 cm

SUMMER

Summer is the warmest season of the year.

HOTTING UP

In summer, everything is bursting with life. Bees buzz about, birds chirp and chatter in the trees, and flowers bloom in the hot sun. June, July and August are the summer months in the Northern Hemisphere. In the Southern Hemisphere, summer is in December, January and February.

What do you call a snowman in July?

A puddle! Ha ha!

HEY, WHAT AM I?

This fuzzy insect is very busy in summer. What is it?
Answer on page 28.

SUMMER SUN

The weather in summer is often hot and sunny. Some days have a gentle **breeze**, but other days are very still and **humid**. As well as hot sunshine, summer can bring dramatic storms with thunder and lightning.

MIDSUMMER

Long summer days are perfect for picnics! The longest day of the year is called the **summer solstice**, or midsummer.

STAYING SAFE

It feels great to play outside in the sunshine, but it's important to stay safe. Always wear sun cream to stop your skin from burning. Drink lots of water to stay **hydrated**.

AUTUMN

In autumn, the days get shorter and the weather gets colder.

WINDING DOWN

Autumn is another season of change. The temperature gets cooler, and the Sun sets a little earlier each day. The leaves on **deciduous trees** change colour and fall to the ground.

WOW!

Until the 1500s, autumn was called 'harvest', because it is the time of year when people would harvest their crops.

MISTS AND FROSTS

Some autumn days are very clear and sunny. After a clear night in late autumn, the ground might be covered by sparkling frost. Other autumn days can be grey, wet and windy. Sometimes in the mornings and evenings, there is fog or mist in the air.

Frosty leaves are caused by ice crystals forming when the temperature falls below freezing point.

HEY, WHAT AM I?

You often see this vegetable in autumn. What is it? Answer on page 28.

HIDE and SEEK

There is an equinox in autumn, as well as in spring. Can you spot a sun and a moon hiding? Answer on page 28.

WINTER

Winter is the coldest season of the year.

COLD AND DARK

In winter, there are fewer animals to be seen, and deciduous trees are bare of leaves. The nights are long and the temperature is colder. December, January and February are the winter months in the Northern Hemisphere. In the Southern Hemisphere, winter is in June, July and August.

HIDE AND SEEK

Can you spot four snowflakes hiding? Answer on page 28.

LET IT SNOW

Winter weather is cold, even when the Sun is shining. On very cold winter days, water droplets in the air become ice and fall to the ground as snow.

When is sunrise?

In about three months!

Changes in the number of daylight hours are more extreme close to the Earth's poles. During winter at the North Pole, the Sun doesn't rise at all for 11 weeks!

HEY, WHAT AM I?

Dripping water can freeze when the temperature drops below zero degrees Celsius. What can you see in this picture?
Answer on page 29.

17

YOUR TURN!

MAKE FROST

See how frost forms on cold surfaces with this super cool experiment. You'll need:

An empty tin can

Some crushed ice (see step one)

Some water

Table salt

STEP ONE

Ask an adult to help you make crushed ice, by wrapping ice cubes in a cloth or bag and crushing them with something heavy, such as a rolling pin. Half-fill the tin can with crushed ice. Add four tablespoons of table salt and a splash of water. Mix well.

Be careful of sharp tin edges!

STEP TWO

Let the tin sit for a few minutes. Watch it while you wait, and you will see frost forming on the part of the tin where the ice and salt mixture is cooling the metal.

STEP THREE

Think about the frost on your can, and the frost that forms outside in autumn and winter. Where do you think it comes from? Why do you think it forms? Answer on page 29.

Animal behaviour changes with the seasons.

NEW LIFE

Spring is the season when most animals have babies. Birds build nests and raise chicks. Insects such as bumblebees wake up out of a very deep sleep, called **hibernation**. They begin to **reproduce** in spring.

THE HIGH LIFE

In summer, there is a lot of food around. **Migratory** animals and birds that spent the winter elsewhere arrive in summer to enjoy the warm weather and tasty plants and insects.

Mosquitoes... yum yum!

STOCKING UP

Autumn is a time to prepare for the winter. Animals such as squirrels collect nuts and store them to get them through the winter ahead. Migratory birds and animals leave to go back to warmer countries.

HIDE AND SEEK

Can you spot five nuts that a squirrel has hidden? Answer on page 29.

WINTER SLEEP

The weather is cold, and there is less food in winter. Some animals, such as dormice, go into hibernation. They spend the whole winter asleep in their cosy nests.

YOUR TURN!

BUILD A BUG HOTEL
Provide insects with a place to hibernate with this crafty science activity. You'll need:

Scissors

A ball of string

Some empty tin cans OR empty plastic bottles

Lots of natural materials such as twigs, pinecones, lengths of bamboo, stones and bark

STEP ONE

If you are using plastic bottles for your bug hotel, cut the tops off.

Ask an adult to help you with the cutting!

STEP TWO

Fill your tins or cut-down plastic bottles with your natural materials. Pack them in tightly, creating small nooks and crannies for bugs to squeeze in between.

Be careful of sharp tin edges!

STEP THREE

Using the string, tie your filled tins or bottles together. You can then either hang your finished bug hotel from a tree, or place it on the ground. Depending on where you put it, you will attract different insect guests.

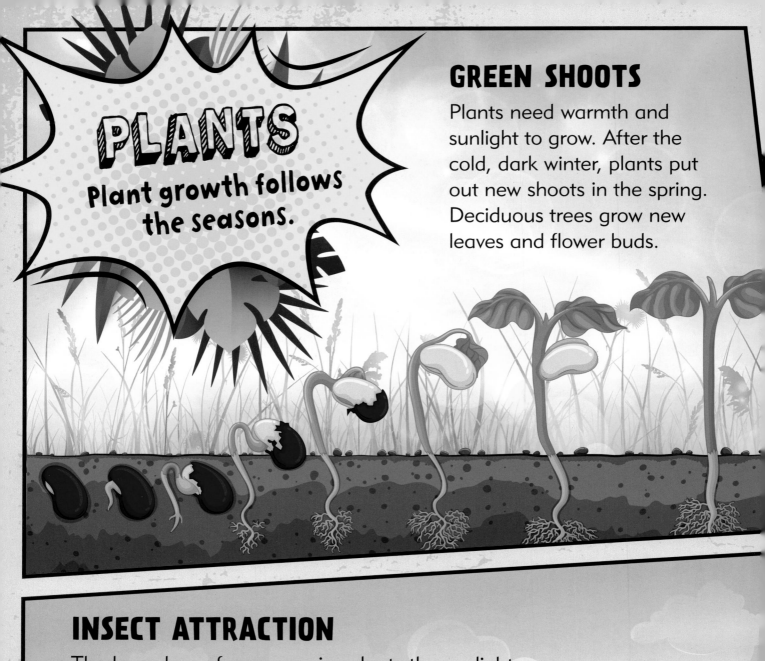

PLANTS
Plant growth follows the seasons.

GREEN SHOOTS

Plants need warmth and sunlight to grow. After the cold, dark winter, plants put out new shoots in the spring. Deciduous trees grow new leaves and flower buds.

INSECT ATTRACTION

The long days of summer give plants the sunlight they need to grow. Flowers bloom, attracting busy insects. Travelling insects **pollinate** the flowers, helping the plants to reproduce.

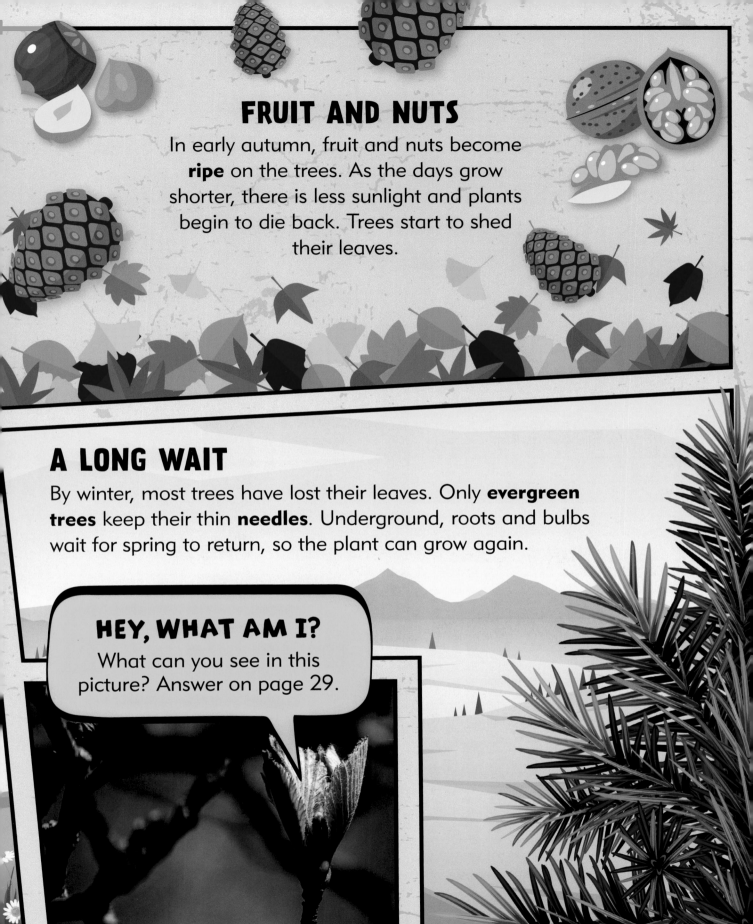

FRUIT AND NUTS

In early autumn, fruit and nuts become **ripe** on the trees. As the days grow shorter, there is less sunlight and plants begin to die back. Trees start to shed their leaves.

A LONG WAIT

By winter, most trees have lost their leaves. Only **evergreen trees** keep their thin **needles**. Underground, roots and bulbs wait for spring to return, so the plant can grow again.

HEY, WHAT AM I?

What can you see in this picture? Answer on page 29.

CELEBRATIONS

Around the world, people celebrate the seasons in different ways.

SPRING RETURNS

Many **cultures** around the world celebrate the arrival of spring. In Japan, cherry blossom parties are held to celebrate the arrival of the pretty spring flowers.

FUN IN SUMMER

In Sweden, the longest day of the year is celebrated with a midsummer **festival**. People dance around **maypoles** and wear crowns made of flowers.

HALLOWEEN

In the past, **Celtic people** celebrated **Samhain**. It was the end of the harvest, and the start of the darker half of the year. It was believed to be a night when ghosts returned to the land of the living! This **tradition** has changed over time to become Halloween in some countries.

WINTER CHEER

Having a feast and a celebration in the middle of winter is a tradition found in many countries. In the Northern Hemisphere, Christmas is a holiday that is celebrated close to midwinter. However, in the Southern Hemisphere, Christmas falls in the middle of summer!

Ho Ho Ho, dudes!

ANSWERS

Page 9

Hide and Seek A rainbow

Page 12

What am I? I'm a bumblebee.

Page 15

What am I? I'm a pumpkin

Page 15

Hide and Seek Sun and moon

Page 16

Hide and Seek Snowflakes

Page 17

What am I? I'm icicles on a building.

Page 21 **Hide and Seek** Nuts

Page 19

Your turn Frost

Frost forms on the side of the can because there is always some water in the air. We just can't see it. When the water in the air touches the very cold can, the water droplets freeze and turn into frost on the side of the can. A similar thing happens with frost outside. Grass and leaves get very cold in the cold weather. When water in the air touches the leaves, it forms frost.

Page 25

What am I? I'm new leaves growing on a tree branch in spring.

GLOSSARY

breeze a gentle wind

Celtic people a group of people who lived in ancient Britain, Ireland and parts of France

culture a group of people with particular beliefs and ways of living

deciduous trees trees that lose their leaves during winter

equinox a date in the year when the day and the night last the same number of hours

evergreen trees trees that do not lose their leaves in winter

festival a time or event of celebration

hibernation when animals go into a deep sleep during the cold winter season

humid when the air is holding a lot of water

hydrated to have had enough water to drink

maypole a tall pole decorated with flowers and ribbons for dancing around

migratory animals that travel long distances each year to find food or places to raise young

needles the thin pointy leaves that some types of tree have, such as pine trees

North Pole the most northern point on the Earth

Northern Hemisphere the part of the Earth that is north of the equator

pollinate when insects carry pollen from one flower to another, which helps the flowers reproduce

reproduce to have offspring or young

ripe fruit that is fully grown and ready to be eaten

Samhain a Celtic celebration that marked the end of harvest and the beginning of winter

Southern Hemisphere the part of the Earth that is south of the equator

summer solstice the date during the year when the night is shortest and the day is longest

tradition a belief or an activity that started in the past and has been carried on

INDEX

KU-027-870

Metals

Plastics

Systems and Controls

Exam-style Questions

Freehand Sketching

Technique and Design Sketches

1 Which of the following statements describe valid reasons for producing a sketch? Tick the **two** correct options.

A To help visualise the 3D appearance of the final product ⬭

B To test whether the product works ⬭

C To fill some spare time ⬭

D To work quickly ⬭

E To experiment with different viewpoints ⬭

F To avoid producing models and written work ⬭

2 The table contains the names of four sketching systems.

Match descriptions **A, B, C** and **D** with the systems **1–4** in the table. Enter the appropriate number in the boxes provided.

	Type of Sketch
1	Isometric sketching
2	Freehand sketching
3	Exploded sketching
4	Orthographic sketching

A Using the eye to judge the correct sizes and angles ⬭

B Sketching a front, side and plan view ⬭

C Sketching parts that aren't fully assembled so the joint details can be seen ⬭

D Sketching at approximately 30° to the left and right of a centre line ⬭

3 Why is it important to produce simple 'crates' when sketching? Tick the correct option.

A You'll be able to draw difficult shapes by building up a collection of simple ones ⬭

B It makes the picture look more colourful ⬭

C It helps you to get the correct proportions ⬭

D It's easier than drawing a complicated picture from scratch ⬭

4 Circle the correct options in the following sentences.

a) Isometric drawings are useful for giving **two-dimensional / three-dimensional** images.

b) Orthographic drawings are useful for giving **two-dimensional / three-dimensional** images.

ONE WEEK LOAN

ESSENTIALS

GCSE Design & Technology
Resistant Materials
Workbook

Contents

Information, Rendered and Textured Sketches

1 (Circle) the correct option in the following sentence.

Information sketches should be drawn **two-dimensionally / three-dimensionally** so that the important details are shown.

2 Draw the following freehand 3D shapes.

a) Square prism

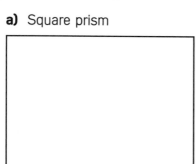

b) Cylinder

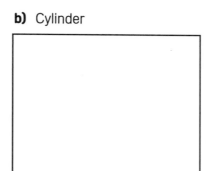

c) Triangular prism

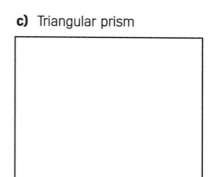

3 Render the outline sketch below to make it look like a piece of wood.

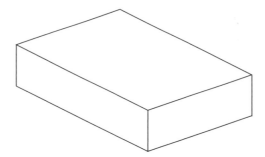

4 Which of the following techniques are suitable for giving images a decorative appearance in an examination? Tick the **two** correct options.

A Colour pencil rendering

B Watercolour paint

C Black ink

D Poster paint

E Soft graphite pencil shading

Working Drawings

Orthographic Detail Drawings and Sketches

1 Give three advantages of using orthographic projection to send information to a manufacturer.

a) ....

b) ....

c) ....

2 Complete the drawing shown and give its full title.

Name of drawing:

....

3 Give three pieces of information that an orthographic sketch can show.

a) ....

b) ....

c) ....

4 Choose the correct words from the options given to complete the following sentences.

clear **colourful** **dimensions** **sectional** **side** **top** **exploded**

It's important that all design drawings are .... and accurate with enough

.... for manufacture to take place.

.... views allow the client to see what happens inside the design.

An .... drawing will give more information.

Modelling, CAD and CAM

Prototype, 3D and Virtual Modelling

1 Which of the following statements describe valid reasons for producing a model? Tick the **two** correct options.

A   To help visualise the 3D appearance of the final product ◯

B   To test whether the product works ◯

C   To experiment with difficult materials and processes ◯

D   To avoid producing drawings and written work ◯

2 The table contains the names of four materials that can be used for modelling.

Match descriptions **A**, **B**, **C** and **D** with the materials **1–4** in the table. Enter the appropriate number in the boxes provided.

A   Manufactured fibreboard, with no grain, that is easier to shape and join than wood ◯

B   Two sheets of thin card with a layer of plastic foam in between them ◯

C   A soft hardwood that can easily be cut and shaped with a craft knife ◯

D   A dense polystyrene foam that can be cut, moulded and joined easily ◯

	Material
1	Styrofoam
2	Balsawood
3	Foam board
4	MDF

The Internet and CAD Packages

3 Choose the correct words from the options given to complete the following sentences.

virtual   computer numeric control   computer   computer aided design

numerical   computer aided manufacture

Software, such as ProDesktop, allows a designer to draw directly onto a .... and

create .... 3D images. This is known as .... , and it also

creates the .... code needed to drive a range of .... machinery.

4 Give three advantages to a designer of using CAD to send information to a manufacturer.

a) ....

b) ....

c) ....

◯

CAD Packages and CAM

How CAM works

1 Give two advantages to a manufacturer of using computer aided manufacture to prototype a product.

a) ....

b) ....

2 What are the three axis that control a CNC machine known as?

....

3 Why would a manufacturer choose to make their products on a computer controlled system? Tick the **three** correct options.

A It's slow to make ◯	**B** Receiving plans by email is easy ◯
C Production is very fast ◯	**D** It's difficult to change size or shape ◯
E Very accurate details can be cut ◯	**F** The workforce will be happy ◯
G Each piece will be slightly different ◯	

Two, Three and Four-axis Machines

4 Give two examples of two-axis machines that are used in schools.

a) ....

b) ....

5 Give two examples of three-axis machines that are used in schools.

a) ....

b) ....

Rapid Prototyping

6 Why would an industrial designer make use of rapid prototyping? Tick the **two** correct options.

A It's a way of manufacturing 2D objects ◯

B It's a way of manufacturing 3D objects ◯

C It's a way of manufacturing a production run ◯

D It's a way of manufacturing using layers of wax that look realistic ◯

Signs

1 The table contains the types of safety signs that could be displayed in a workshop.

Match descriptions **A, B, C** and **D** with the safety signs **1–4** in the table. Enter the appropriate number in the boxes provided.

Safety Signs	
1	Round red
2	Round blue
3	Triangular yellow
4	Rectangular green

A A specific behaviour or action that must be carried out, e.g. wear personal protective equipment ☐

B Dangerous behaviour that you must avoid doing, e.g. don't smoke ☐

C Escape routes, equipment and facilities, e.g. fire exit or first aid box ☐

D Be careful or take precautions, e.g. dangerous chemicals or spills ☐

2 What do the following safety symbols mean?

a) _____

b) _____

COSHH

3 What does COSHH stand for?

_____

4 Why would a manufacturer insist that the workforce work safely in a workshop? Tick the **two** correct options.

A It reduces costs ☐

B It's a legal requirement ☐

C The health and safety of the workers is important ☐

D It will increase the productivity of the workforce ☐

☐

Health and Safety

1 Choose the correct words from the options given to complete the following sentences.

gauntlets   metal dustbin   ear protectors   goggles   dust extraction
heating   scrap   cupboard   gloves

When working in a wood machining area it's essential that _____ are worn to protect

the ears and _____ are used for the face. The _____ system

should be switched on and any _____ wood should be placed in a

_____ so that there's no chance of an accidental fire.

2 Give two safety precautions that you should take when turning a piece of wood on a lathe.

a) _____

b) _____

3 Give three safety checks that you should make before using a drilling machine.

a) _____

b) _____

c) _____

Hazards and Protecting Yourself

4 When brazing a copper tube, the metal becomes very hot and toxic fumes are given off. What
precautions should you take to protect yourself?

_____

5 When using solvent cement, the material and fumes given off are toxic. What precautions should you take
to protect yourself?

_____

6 When spray-painting steel, toxic fumes are given off and there's a danger of overspray. What precautions
should you take to protect yourself?

_____

Health and Safety

Welding, Brazing and Gluing Plastics

1 Suggest three safety precautions that you should take when heating metal in a hearth.

....

....

2 Which of the following statements describe valid reasons for taking care when working with solvents to weld plastics? Tick the **two** correct options.

A The fumes are toxic if they're breathed in ☐

B The solvent is toxic and can damage the skin ☐

C Heat is always given off when using solvents ☐

D Solvents will not weld plastics ☐

Chemical Sprays and Storage

3 What does the following safety symbol mean?

....

Working with Heat and Chemicals

4 Explain the meaning of each of the following symbols and give a process or piece of machinery where you might expect to see the sign.

a) ....

....

b) ....

....

c) ....

....

d) ....

Designers and Styles

1 Who was Charles Rennie Mackintosh? Tick the correct option.

A An American architect, interior designer and writer of Welsh descent ⬭

B A Scottish architect, designer and water colourist ⬭

C A French designer who was probably the best known designer in the New Design style ⬭

D A Italian architect and designer of the late 20th Century ⬭

2 Who was Ettore Sottsass? Tick the correct option.

A An American architect, interior designer and writer of Welsh descent ⬭

B A Scottish architect, designer and water colourist ⬭

C A French designer who was probably the best known designer in the New Design style ⬭

D A Italian architect and designer of the late 20th Century ⬭

3 What product is James Dyson famous for designing?

_____

In the Style of...

4 Which movement started in Germany in 1919 and combined the crafts and fine arts? Tick the correct option.

A Memphis ⬭   **B** Art Deco ⬭

C Shaker ⬭   **D** Art Nouveau ⬭

E Bauhaus ⬭   **F** De Stijl ⬭

5 Which Dutch movement, founded in 1917, was formed on the artistic philosophy of 'new plastic art'? Tick the correct option.

A Memphis ⬭   **B** Art Deco ⬭

C Shaker ⬭   **D** Art Nouveau ⬭

E Bauhaus ⬭   **F** De Stijl ⬭

6 Which movement (1890–1905) was characterised by organic motifs, especially those inspired by plants and flowers? Tick the correct option.

A Memphis ⬭   **B** Art Deco ⬭

C Shaker ⬭   **D** Art Nouveau ⬭

E Bauhaus ⬭   **F** De Stijl ⬭

Social, Moral and Environmental Issues

Raw Materials

1 Which of the following statements describe valid reasons for designers looking after the environment?
Tick the **two** correct options.

A   To help understand how animals live ◯

B   To see if there will be enough coal left in 50 years' time ◯

C   To ensure that there will be enough natural resources left for future generations ◯

D   To prevent people from working in factories ◯

E   To stop the destruction of rainforests ◯

F   To avoid having to dig up any more minerals ◯

Finite Resources

2 Match descriptions **A, B, C** and **D** with the energy sources **1–4** in the table. Enter the appropriate number in the boxes provided.

A   Plant remains that have been changed by pressure over time into a rock ◯

B   Growing plants that can be processed to become fuel ◯

C   Plant remains that have been changed by pressure over time into a thick liquid ◯

D   Radioactive materials that give off great heat when they're processed ◯

	Energy Source
1	Coal
2	Oil
3	Nuclear
4	Bio fuel

Ethical Employers and Carbon Footprint

3 Name two conditions that an ethical employer would ensure that their workers benefit from.

a) ....

b) ....

4 Explain what the following words mean.

a) Carbon capture: ....

b) Finite resource: ....

c) Sustainability: ....

◯

Social, Moral and Environmental Issues

The 6 Rs

1 Circle the correct options in the following sentences.

a) An old machine will be **recycled / re-used** if it's dismantled and the parts are used again.

b) An old machine will be **recycled / re-used** if it's melted down and the materials are used again.

2 Complete the table below.

Process	Description	Explanation
Reduce	a) _____	This will reduce the amount of natural resources used and save energy
Repair	Products that break should be repaired rather than thrown out	b) _____
Recycle	c) _____	This will reduce the amount of material put into landfill sites and reduce the use of raw materials
Refuse	Environmentally friendly designs should be used instead of unethical or wasteful designs	d) _____

Maintenance and Sustainability

3 a) Explain why solid wood is considered to be environmentally friendly.

_____

b) Explain why plastic is **not** considered to be environmentally friendly.

_____

4 Which of the following are valid reasons for **not** using excessive packaging? Tick the **three** correct options.

A   Packaging looks unsightly if it's thrown away ◯

B   Packaging fills up landfill sites ◯

C   Packaging makes the contents look better ◯

D   Packaging can cause harm to wildlife ◯

E   Packaging protects the contents ◯

Cultural and Moral Issues

Human Factors, Inclusive and Exclusive Design

1 Circle the correct options in the following sentences.

The ideal product is one that meets everyone's needs. This is called **inclusive / exclusive** design and designers try to **exclude / include** as few people as possible.

Inclusive / Exclusive designs focus on **specific groups / just women.** Designers have a **need / responsibility** to ensure that nothing they design will offend the people who will use the products.

2 Suggest the different factors you would need to consider if you were designing a waterproof jacket for a man and a waterproof jacket for a dog.

....

....

....

3 Name three human factors that a designer needs to include when thinking about a design.

a) ....

b) ....

c) ....

Stereotypes, Offence and Ethical Trading

4 Why are stereotypes used when designing products?

....

5 Why would a designer need to carry out extensive research on a product in terms of cultural issues?

....

6 What do ethical traders try to do? Tick the **two** correct options.

A Make a lot of money to improve the economy ⬭

B Consider the welfare of the planet and the people who live on it ⬭

C Use finite resources ⬭

D Work towards a sustainable future ⬭

Anthropometric Data

Anthropometrics and Ergonomics

1 Explain what an ergonome is.

....

2 Choose the correct words from the options given to complete the following sentences.

safety   hundreds   80%   comfort   90%

charts   boxes   45%   millions

The collection of human measurements, which have been taken from .... of people

and put together in ...., is called anthropometric data. Designers try to cater for

.... of the population and use this data to deal with issues such as

.... and ....

3 Circle the correct options in the following sentences.

     a) **Anthropometrics / Ergonomics** is the study of human measurements.

     b) **Anthropometrics / Ergonomics** is the study of the efficiency of people in their working environment.

The Design Cast List

4 The table contains the names of four people involved in the design process.

Match descriptions **A, B, C** and **D** with the people **1−4**
in the table. Enter the appropriate number in the boxes provided.

	People
1	Manufacturer
2	Designer
3	Client
4	User

     A   Someone who comes up with ideas for the new product   ◯

     B   Someone who specialises in certain types of production   ◯

     C   Someone who buys or has access to the product   ◯

     D   Someone who commissions a piece of work   ◯

5 What important pieces of information might a designer need to collect from their client if they're designing a jewellery box? Tick the **three** correct options.

     A   The client's height   ◯

     B   The number of rings the client has to store   ◯

     C   The type of material the client prefers for making the box   ◯

     D   The client's favourite earrings   ◯

     E   The size of the client's longest necklace   ◯

Anthropometric Data & Scales of Production

The Design Cast List (Cont.)

1 Why is advertising important?

....

....

2 Why is market research important?

....

....

3 List three ways in which a manufacturer can carry out market research.

a) ....   b) ....   c) ....

4 List three ways in which a manufacturer can advertise their products.

a) ....   b) ....   c) ....

Production Systems

5 Choose the correct words from the options given to complete the following sentences.

component   **warehousing**   **continuous**   **more**

just-in-time   **interrupted**   **broken**   **batch**   **less**

.... production involves the arrival of .... parts at exactly the

time they are needed at the factory. This system uses .... storage space so saves

on costly ...., But, if the supply of components is stopped, the production line is

...., which then becomes very costly.

6 What do mass production systems always make use of? Tick the **two** correct options.

A 24/7 working ⬭

B A production line where different workers are responsible for different jobs ⬭

C Batches of thousands of the same product being made ⬭

D Quality control ⬭

Quality Assurance Systems

Quality Assurance and Quality Control

1 Circle the correct options in the following sentences.

a) Ensuring the accuracy of products before and during manufacture are quality **control / assurance** issues.

b) Checks carried out during manufacture are quality **control / assurance** issues.

2 Choose the correct words from the options given to complete the following sentences.

testing	**measuring**	**thickness**	**smell**
	diameter	**taste**	**screws**

Sampling is an important part of the .... of a manufactured product and can take

place at any time during production.

An injection-moulded plastic bottle top could be tested for .... and

.... and to check whether it .... onto its container properly.

3 In what ways can members of the public be involved in monitoring products? Tick the **two** correct options.

A By complaining when something goes wrong ◯

B By filling in questionnaires ◯

C By deliberately being sold broken products so that they'll return them ◯

D By working in a factory for a day to see how difficult it is ◯

Tolerances

4 When products are produced in large quantities, it's very hard to guarantee that each one will meet the specifications accurately, so a tolerance has to be accepted. Explain what is meant by **tolerance**.

....

....

....

....

Quality Assurance Systems

Accuracy

1 When would you use a holding device? Tick the **two** correct options.

    A   When checking materials for the right quality   ◯

    B   When drilling accurate holes in components   ◯

    C   When cutting materials to the correct size   ◯

    D   When screwing bolts into holes   ◯

Jigs and Fixtures

2 What is a sawing jig used for? Tick the correct option.

    A   Accurately sawing at a variety of angles   ◯

    B   Accurately cutting angles of 45°   ◯

    C   Accurately cutting edges   ◯

    D   Accurately sawing a variety of different widths   ◯

3 What is a mitre box used for? Tick the correct option.

    A   Accurately sawing at a variety of angles   ◯

    B   Accurately cutting angles of 45°   ◯

    C   Accurately cutting edges   ◯

    D   Accurately sawing a variety of different widths   ◯

4 What is the difference between a fixture and a jig?

....

5 What is the purpose of a sawing fence on a band saw?

....

6 Sketch a drilling jig suitable for making a hole in the corner of a piece of acrylic.

Flow Charts

1 Complete the table below.

Symbol	Name	What Does it Mean?
▭	a)	b)
c)	Terminator (start / stop)	The flow chart must start and stop with a terminator
d)	Decision	e)
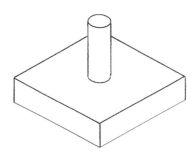	f)	If a process hasn't been carried out correctly, e.g. the wood is too short, the feedback tells the operator what to do next

2 This is a sketch of a dowel joint. Choose the correct processes from the options given to complete the flow chart below. Put the appropriate number in the boxes provided.

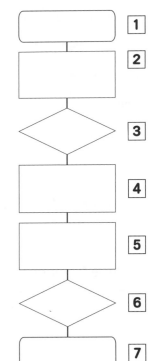

A   Start

B   Check the accuracy of the marking out

C   Mark out the hole

D   Glue the dowel

E   Finish

F   Drill the hole

G   Check the dowel is square

Measuring and Checking

Accuracy

1 Which of the following statements describe valid reasons for checking the accuracy of marking out work before cutting? Tick the **two** correct options.

A To save time by not having to re-cut the work ◯

B To go over the lines to make them darker ◯

C To spend time thinking about things ◯

D To make sure that all the parts will fit together ◯

2 Why is it important to use millimetres rather than inches when marking out? Tick the correct option.

A Because they're more accurate ◯   B Because it's traditional ◯

C Because they're the correct SI unit ◯   D Because they're smaller ◯

Rules, Micrometers, Gauges and Spirit Levels

3 The table contains the names of four tools that can be used for measuring.

Match descriptions **A**, **B**, **C** and **D** with the tools **1–4** in the table. Enter the appropriate number in the boxes provided.

A Used to measure the outside or the inside of circular bars and tubes ◯

	Tool
1	Spirit level
2	Micrometer
3	Caliper
4	Steel rule

B A ratchet mechanism prevents the jaws being pressed too hard and it's accurate up to 0.01 mm ◯

C A simple steel bar with divisions engraved along the edge used to measure lengths ◯

D Used for checking horizontal and vertical surfaces. The bubble in the tube must fall within the markings ◯

4 Circle the correct options in the following sentences.

a) A micrometer is usually used for measuring **inside and outside / outside** dimensions.

b) A Vernier gauge can be used for measuring **inside and outside / outside** dimensions.

5 Which of the following types of square are suitable for checking the outside angle of a square box for 90°? Tick the **two** correct options.

A Set square ◯   B Tri square ◯

C Engineering square ◯   D Tee square ◯

E Angle square ◯

Measuring and Checking

Measuring

1 Choose the correct words from the options given to complete the following sentences.

ruler	identical	checks	measure	quality
	quantity	gauges	gouges	

You may need to manufacture _____ items, for example, parts of a child's toy. To

ensure that each part is the same, you'll need to undertake measuring _____ as part

of the _____ assurance procedures using _____ or measuring

devices.

Sticks, Gauges and Measuring Devices

2 List the three tools you would need if you wanted to mark a wall in order to put up a picture.

a) _____ b) _____ c) _____

3 Circle the correct options in the following sentences.

a) A **gap / marking** gauge is a checking tool used to make sure that components are the correct size.

b) A **gap / marking** gauge is a tool used to mark parallel lines on a piece of wood.

4 Describe how you would check the squareness of a frame without using a square to measure the corner angles.

_____

_____

_____

5 Name two very sophisticated forms of technologies that are used to measure and check dimensions.

a) _____

b) _____

Vices

1 Why is it important to use a vice when cutting and abrading metals? Tick the **two** correct options.

A It's the way it's always done ⭕

B The piece of metal can slip and cut you if it isn't held firmly ⭕

C If you don't use a vice, you waste effort pushing against yourself ⭕

D If you don't use a vice, the file could slip and cut you ⭕

2 Give one reason why you should use different vices for holding woods and metals.

....

3 The table contains the names of four holding devices. Match descriptions **A**, **B**, **C** and **D** with the materials **1–4** in the table. Enter the appropriate number in the boxes provided.

A Used to hold smaller and irregular pieces of plastic and sheet metal that will not fit into other vices ⭕

B Used for holding materials whilst being drilled or milled on a machine ⭕

C Has wooden jaws and is used to hold timber and plastics to the workbench whilst they're being cut ⭕

D Raised above the workbench and is available with hard steel jaws ⭕

	Holding Device
1	Engineering vice
2	Machine vice
3	Hand vice
4	Woodworking vice

Cramps

4 Complete the table below.

Name	Image of Cramp	Description
a)		b)
c)		d)
e)		f)
g)		Uses a self-locking system, which makes the positioning easier than with a conventional cramp ⭕

Hammering

Hammers

1 The table contains the names of three types of hammer. Match descriptions **A, B** and **C** with the hammers **1–3** in the table. Enter the appropriate number in the boxes provided.

A A general purpose hammer that gets its name from its wedge-shaped rear face, which is used to start small nails ◯

B Has a rounded rear face used for spreading or rounding rivet heads ◯

C A heavy hammer that can be used to remove bent nails and drive large nails through timber ◯

	Hammer
1	Claw hammer
2	Ball pein hammer
3	Cross pein hammer

2 Why wouldn't you use a claw hammer to start a small nail?

....

....

3 Why wouldn't you use a planishing hammer for general metalwork?

....

....

Mallets

4 Which of the following statements describe valid reasons for using a mallet? Tick the **two** correct options.

A A mallet makes less noise than a hammer ◯

B A mallet is cheaper to buy than a hammer ◯

C A mallet won't damage the end of a chisel if it's used to hit it ◯

D A mallet won't damage the surface of a piece of metal if it's used to hit it ◯

5 Circle the correct options in the following sentences.

a) A **nylon / bossing** mallet is the modern equivalent of the traditional beech mallet. It can be used for assembling wood joints as well as bending over sheet metals without damaging the surface.

b) A **nylon / bossing** mallet is made with an egg-shaped boxwood head. It's used with a leather sandbag for hollowing or dishing sheet metal.

Properties and Environmental Issues

Choosing a Material

1 Match descriptions **A, B, C, D, E** and **F** with the properties **1–6** in the table. Enter the appropriate number in the boxes provided.

	Material Property
1	Tensile strength
2	Shear
3	Durability
4	Ductility
5	Compressive strength
6	Brittleness

A Resisting strong sliding forces acting opposite to each other ☐

B The ability to be stretched and permanently deformed without breaking ☐

C Very strong under pressure ☐

D Withstanding force when stretched ☐

E Will break easily without bending. The opposite of ductile ☐

F Withstanding wear and tear, and weathering ☐

2 Circle the correct options in the following sentences.

a) Materials that allow electricity to pass through easily are said to be **thermally / electrically** conductive.

b) Materials that allow heat to pass through easily are said to be **thermally / electrically** conductive.

Wood

3 Circle the correct options in the following sentences.

a) Wood is a **renewable / recyclable** resource that can be replaced by replanting trees.

b) Wood is a **renewable / recyclable** resource that can be re-used by dismantling end-of-life products.

4 Choose the correct words from the options given to complete the following sentences.

trunks   atmosphere   replaced   roots

rots   renewed   recycled

Trees store carbon in their _____. If the wood _____ or burns, this

carbon is released into the _____. So, rather than being burned, wood products

should be _____ into chip board or MDF. ☐

Properties and Environmental Issues

Metals

1 Why is it important to recycle metals, rather than mining new ores from the ground? Tick the **two** correct options.

    A It will make people appreciate the metals more   ◯

    B There are health and safety issues with the working conditions
       of the miners digging in dangerous places and breathing in dust   ◯

    C Ores need to be smelted, a process that gives off toxic fumes   ◯

    D The used ores are much stronger   ◯

2 Choose the correct words from the options given to complete the following sentences.

    energy   **oxygen**   **non-renewable**   **five**   **carbon dioxide**

                        copper ore   **aluminium ore**

The heat energy required to smelt and shape metals usually comes from burning

_____ fossil fuels, which give off toxic fumes and release _____

into the atmosphere. So, recycling metals is important to preserve our limited resources, and reduce the

amount of _____ needed to work the metals.

Plastics

3 What environmental problems are there with using plastics that might make them an issue for a designer? Tick the **three** correct options.

    A Most plastics can be recycled   ◯

    B Most plastics are made from oil, which is a non-renewable resource   ◯

    C Many people prefer natural materials like wood   ◯

    D Growing plants to provide bio-material for plastics uses land that
       could have been used for growing food   ◯

    E Plastic production produces toxic by-products that have to be disposed of   ◯

4 Give three reasons why it's important to recycle plastic materials.

    a) _____

    b) _____

    c) _____

Woods

Timber and its Natural Characteristics

1 Match descriptions **A**, **B** and **C** with the woods **1–3** in the table.
Enter the appropriate number in the boxes provided.

	Wood
1	Hardwood
2	Softwood
3	Manufactured board

A Timber sheets that are made by gluing together either wood layers or wood fibres ◯

B Come from slow-growing, deciduous or broad-leafed trees ◯

C Come from fast-growing, coniferous or needle-leafed trees ◯

2 Which of the following properties are advantages when using manufactured board? Tick the **two** correct options.

A It has a beautiful grain ◯

B It's available in large sheets ◯

C It's much cheaper than solid wood ◯

D It's unlikely to warp ◯

3 Sketch a piece of plywood to show the way in which it's made.

4 Give a definition (description) for each of the following terms:

a) Grain pattern: ....

b) Workability: ....

c) Structural strength: ....

5 Choose the correct words from the options given to complete the following sentences.

along   fibres   length   mahogany   annual rings
width   across   balsawood

Wood is made from .... that run along the length of a tree. They are grown in

groups that make up .... The wood will split easily along the

.... of the fibres, but it must be cut or sawn .... the grain.

Softwoods are usually softer to work than most hardwoods, but some hardwoods can be light

and soft, for example, ...

Woods

Hardwoods

1 Describe, in as much detail as you can, the properties of beech.

_____

_____

2 Give three uses for ash.

a) _____

b) _____

c) _____

3 Describe, in as much detail as you can, the properties of teak.

_____

_____

4 Match the uses **A**, **B**, **C** and **D** with the woods **1–4** in the table.
Enter the appropriate number in the boxes provided.

A An outdoor table ◯

B A child's toy ◯

C A hockey stick ◯

D An indoor dining table ◯

	Wood
1	Ash
2	Mahogany
3	Teak
4	Beech

5 a) Why are thin layers of hardwood often glued onto manufactured boards such as MDF?

_____

b) What is the name given to this technique?

_____

Woods

Softwoods

1 Complete the table below.

Wood	Description	Uses
Scots pine	Straight-grained but knotty. Light in colour. Fairly strong, but easy to work with. Cheap.	**a)** ....
Parana pine	**b)**	High quality pine furniture and fittings.
c)	Light in weight and knot-free. Reddish brown and naturally oily. Easy to work with.	**d)** ....
Pitch pine	**e)**	Furniture and church pews.
Yew	Rich red-brown with small hard knots. Very durable.	**f)** ....

2 Match the uses **A, B, C** and **D** with the woods **1–4** in the table. Enter the appropriate number in the boxes provided.

	Wood
1	Cedar
2	Pine
3	Yew
4	Parana pine

A An indoor shelf ◯   **B** A fence ◯

C Kitchen cupboards ◯   **D** A staircase ◯

3 Which of the following properties makes cedar a good timber to choose for the timber cladding of buildings? Tick the **two** correct options.

A It has a beautiful deep reddish-brown colour ◯   **B** It's available in large sheets ◯

C It's much cheaper than hardwood ◯   **D** It's unlikely to warp ◯

E It resists insect and fungal attacks ◯

Manufactured Boards

Manufactured Boards

1 What do the following acronyms stand for?

   a) MDF ....

   b) WBP ....

2 Circle the correct options in the following sentences.

   a) **Plywood / Chip board** is a manufactured board made from waste materials.

   b) **Plywood / Chip board** is a manufactured board made from veneers.

3 Give three advantages of using manufactured boards.

   a) ....

   b) ....

   c) ....

4 Give three disadvantages of using manufactured boards.

   a) ....

   b) ....

   c) ....

5 Give two uses for chip board.

   a) ....

   b) ....

6 Explain why it's necessary to cover the **edges** of manufactured boards.

   ....

7 Give two uses for blockboard.

   a) ....

   b) ....

Marking Out Wood

Measuring Lengths and Angles

1 Match the uses **A, B, C** and **D** with the marking out tools **1–4** in the table. Enter the appropriate number in the boxes provided.

A Used to mark lines exactly at 45° from the edge of the material ◯

B Used to cut the wood fibres before sawing across the grain ◯

C An adjustable angle marker that can be set to any angle ◯

D Used to mark lines exactly at 90° from the edge of the material ◯

	Marking Out Tool
1	Tri square
2	Sliding bevel
3	Mitre square
4	Marking knife

2 a) Describe how you would make and use a template to mark out the curves shown below on the four corners of a piece of wood.

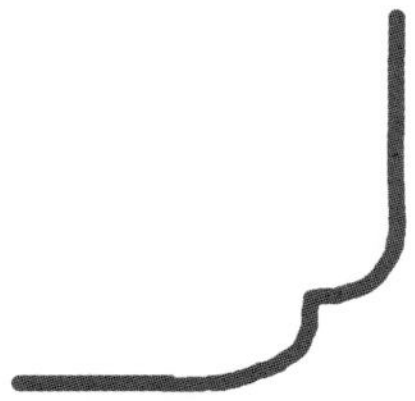

....

....

b) Which tool would be used when marking out the curve? Tick the correct option.

A Marking knife ◯   **B** Square ◯

C Gauge ◯   **D** Pencil ◯

Marking the Surface

3 Why should a knife be used when marking out woods?

....

....

Gauges

4 Which of the following tools is suitable for marking two parallel lines on wood? Tick the correct option.

A Marking gauge ◯   **B** Cutting gauge ◯

C Mortise gauge ◯   **D** Parallel gauge ◯

Cutting Wood

Chiselling Wood

1 Complete the table below.

Image	Tool name	Description /Uses
	a) _____	A strong, thicker chisel used for chopping deep holes for joints
	Firmer chisel	**b)** _____
	c) _____	**d)** _____
	Bevel-edged chisel	**e)** _____

Basic Chiselling Actions

2 Match the uses **A, B** and **C** with the processes **1–3** in the table.
Enter the appropriate number in the boxes provided.

A Cutting across a joint to clean out waste ⭕

B Digging out waste from a mortise by cutting the fibres into short lengths ⭕

C Pushing down onto a waste surface to shape the end of a piece of wood ⭕

	Process
1	Vertical paring
2	Chopping
3	Horizontal paring

3 Choose the correct words from the options given to complete the following sentences.

crack　　slice　　sharp　　hard　　split　　grain　　blunt　　move

There are four types of wood chisel. A _____ edge is essential for chisels to work

properly as they need to _____ across the _____. If used along

the grain, a chisel will _____ the wood unless it's very sharp.

4 What would happen to a chisel if you were to hit it with the steel face of a hammer?

_____

Planing

1 Choose the correct words from the options given to complete the following sentences.

shave   **across**   **wedge-shaped**   **thick**   **steep**   **along**

Planing works when a .... cutting blade is used to .... off

thin layers of wood. It's important to plane .... the grain. Special planes with a

.... cutting angle allow planing across the end grain.

2 Match the uses **A**, **B**, **C** and **D** with the planes **1–4** in the table. Enter the appropriate number in the boxes provided.

A Used to remove shavings to bring the wood to the right size for working ◯

B Used to finish the surface before using abrasives ◯

C Used for planing end grain ◯

D Used to remove large amounts of wood when sculpting or carving ◯

	Plane
1	Smoothing plane
2	Surform
3	Jack plane
4	Block plane

Drilling

3 Choose the correct names from the options given to state which drill has made each of the three holes. Enter the appropriate number in the boxes provided.

1   2   3

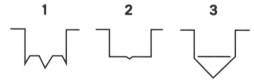

A Forstner bit ◯

B Twist bit ◯

C Auger bit ◯

4 Circle the correct options in the following sentences.

a) Drill bits are usually made from **high carbon / mild** steel.

b) Drill bits rotate **anti-clockwise / clockwise** when drilling.

5 What would a countersink bit be used for? Tick the correct option.

A Making large tapered holes in a piece of wood ◯

B Making small square holes ◯

C Making holes to allow screw heads to finish flush with the surface of the wood ◯

D Making deep flat-bottomed holes in a piece of wood ◯

▢

Cutting Wood

Drilling (Cont.)

1 Choose the correct words from the options given to complete the following sentences.

goggles   **pillar**   **gauntlets**   **drilling**   **hand**   **machine vice**

Pedestal drills are also known as _____ drills and can be bench or floor mounted.

They provide the safest and easiest method of drilling materials that can be lifted onto the

_____ table. When drilling, the material must be firmly held in place by using a

_____ or cramps and the operator must wear _____ and a dust mask.

Sawing Wood and Hand Saws

2 Circle the correct options in the following sentences.

a) A **cross-cut / rip** saw is used when cutting along the grain.

b) A **cross-cut / rip** saw is used when cutting across the grain.

3 Explain how you would cut the shape below from a piece of plywood 50mm x 50mm x 6mm.

_____

_____

_____

Back Saws and Power Saws

4 Match the uses **A, B** and **C** with the saws **1–3** in the table. Enter the appropriate number in the boxes provided.

A   Used to cut out large pieces of wood from sheets   ◯

B   Used to cut joints and small pieces of wood to size   ◯

C   Used to cut around curves   ◯

	Saw
1	Coping saw
2	Hand saw
3	Tenon saw

5 Explain how a machine jigsaw works.

_____

_____

Joining Wood

Joints and Simple Joints

1 Circle the correct options in the following sentences.

A butt joint is **strong / weak** because it has no mechanical properties. There are many traditional joints that can be used to build structural **strength / density** into products. Strength increases with **surface area / width**, so more **solder / glue** equals more strength.

2 Complete the table below.

Joint	Description	Image
a) _____	Involves removing half the material from each piece	b)
Dowel joint	c) _____	d)
e) _____	f) _____	

3 Match the uses **A, B, C** and **D** with the jointing methods **1–4** in the table. Enter the appropriate number in the boxes provided.

A Chair legs and cupboard corners

B Strengthened with nails, and used in frame and carcase joints

C Picture frames

D Cupboard shelves

	Joint
1	Housing joint
2	Dowel joint
3	Mitre joint
4	Lap joint

Complicated Joints

4 What kind of joint is the strongest joint for box constructions? Tick the correct option.

A Mortise and tenon

B Biscuit

C Dovetail

D Dowel

Joining Wood

Temporary Joints

1 Name the three screw heads below.

a) ▼ b) ◢ c) ▼

a) ....

b) ....

c) ....

2 Circle the correct options in the following sentences.

a) A **nail / screw** makes a very weak joint if used on its own.

b) A **nail / screw** can easily be removed and replaced in order to take things apart.

3 What are nailed joints correctly used for? Tick the **two** correct options.

A As a permanent fitting for chair legs ◯

B To hold wooden things together while the glue dries ◯

C As an axle for a toy car ◯

D To fix the backs of cupboards ◯

4 Why are cross head screws more popular than slot head screws? Tick the **two** correct options.

A They're easier to drive in using an electrically powered driver ◯

B They're very strong when used across the grain ◯

C They're useful for fixing other materials, such as metals or plastics, to timber ◯

D They're less likely to slip off the screwdriver ◯

Permanent Joints and Knock-down Fittings

5 Match the fastenings **A, B, C** and **D** with the jointing methods **1–4** in the table.
Enter the appropriate number in the boxes provided.

A A locking system that has a cam that locks the parts together ◯

B A fitting that fits into a hole to provide a threaded insert that takes a machine screw ◯

C Plastic blocks used to take screws in each direction and are suitable for simple joints ◯

D A metal-screwed insert that sits in a hole and takes a machine screw ◯

	Joint
1	Cross dowel
2	Pronged nut
3	Modesty blocks
4	Cam bolt

Adhesives and Finishes

Glue Types

1 Explain why joints are glued.

....

2 Match the descriptions **A, B, C, D** and **E** with the glues **1–5** in the table.
Enter the appropriate number in the boxes provided.

A Ideal for gluing plastic laminates onto chip board ◯

B A white, water-based adhesive ◯

C A waterproof adhesive, which is mixed into
a creamy consistency with water ◯

D Useful for quick modelling ◯

E An adhesive that will stick most clean, dry
materials together ◯

	Glue
1	Polyvinyl acetate
2	Epoxy resin
3	Contact adhesive
4	Hot melt glue
5	Synthetic resin

3 Circle the correct options in the following sentences.

a) **Latex adhesive / Epoxy resin** is a very versatile but expensive adhesive that sets chemically very hard.

b) **Latex adhesive / Epoxy resin** is a rubber solution that is cheap and safe to use.

Abrasive Papers

4 What materials are commonly used as abrasives for wood finishing? Tick the **two** correct options.

A Emery ◯   **B** Sand ◯   **C** Garnet ◯   **D** Glass ◯

5 What material are the abrasives for wood finishing glued onto? Tick the correct option.

A Paper ◯   **B** Cardboard ◯   **C** Wood ◯   **D** Cloth ◯

6 Choose the correct words from the options given to complete the following sentences.

fine   **sieve**   **wooden block**   **garnet**   **cork block**   **flour**

Each abrasive sheet is numbered with the .... size that the abrasive passed

through, so higher numbers are finer abrasives. The papers are graded into coarse, medium and fine

with .... paper being the finest. Glass and .... paper

are used mainly for wood. Abrasive paper is usually wrapped around a ....

to keep it flat.

◯

Surface Finishes

Finishing Wood

1 Why is polish applied to wood? Tick the **four** correct options.

A To protect it from moisture ◯   B To protect it from insect attack ◯

C To make it less attractive ◯   D To enhance the colour of the grain ◯

E To make it easier to wipe the surface clean ◯   F To make it more expensive ◯

2 Which of the following finishes is suitable for a piece of wood to be used outside? Tick the correct option.

A No finish ◯   B Wax polish ◯

C Polyurethane varnish ◯   D Silver polish ◯

3 The table contains the names of five types of wood finish. Match descriptions **A, B, C, D** and **E** with the finishes **1–5** in the table. Enter the appropriate number in the boxes provided.

A Can be used to change the colour of the timber and show up the grain patterns ◯

B Fills the porous surface of the timber. A layer of polish is built up on the surface of the material ◯

C A hard, quick-drying finish useful when wood turning ◯

D A tough, heatproof and waterproof finish available in different colours with a matt, satin or gloss surface finish ◯

E A solvent-based product similar to a varnish, which is used to seal timber ◯

	Finish
1	French polish
2	Cellulose
3	Wax polish
4	Polyurethane varnish
5	Wood stains

4 Which of the following types of finishes are suitable for giving wood surfaces a decorative *and* protective finish? Tick the **two** correct options.

A Gloss paint ◯   B Watercolour paint ◯   C Lacquer ◯   D Emulsion ◯

5 Circle the correct options in the following sentences.

a) Wax is usually applied with a **brush / cloth**.

b) Varnish is usually applied with a **brush / cloth**.

6 The table contains the names of four types of finish.

Match the uses **A, B, C** and **D** with the finishes **1–4** in the table. Enter the appropriate number in the boxes provided.

A An outdoor table ◯   B A child's toy ◯

C A hockey stick ◯   D An indoor dining table ◯

	Finish
1	Linseed oil
2	Gloss paint
3	Acrylic paint
4	French polish

Metals and their Properties

Metals and their Properties

1 Match descriptions **A, B, C, D, E** and **F** with the properties **1–6** in the table. Enter the appropriate number in the boxes provided.

A   The ability to accept bending or distorting   ◯

B   The ability to regain its original shape after it has been deformed   ◯

C   Resistance to scratching, cutting, denting and wear   ◯

D   The ability to be easily pressed, spread and hammered
into shapes   ◯

E   Withstanding force without breaking or bending permanently   ◯

F   A change in the structure of a metal as a result of repeated
hammering or strain   ◯

	Property
1	Hardness
2	Work hardness
3	Flexibility
4	Strength
5	Elasticity
6	Malleability

2 Circle the correct options in the following sentences.

a)   Metals that contain iron are **non-ferrous / alloys / ferrous.**

b)   Metals that contain no iron are **non-ferrous / alloys / ferrous.**

c)   Metals that contain mixtures of metals or elements are **non-ferrous / alloys / ferrous.**

Heat Treatment

3 Choose the correct words from the options given to complete the following sentences.

heating   **work hardened**   **broken**   **brittle**   **soft**

working   **annealed**   **tempered**

After a metal has been deformed by _____ (hammering or bending), it becomes

_____ and if you continue to work the metal it will become _____

or crack. So, the metal needs to be _____ . _____ allows the grains

to re-form and, on cooling, the metal will have returned to its original condition and working can continue.

4 Why is it important to understand how to change the crystalline structure of metals? Tick the **two** correct
options.

A   It allows the metalworker to make the metal softer   ◯

B   It allows the metalworker to spend less time at the forge   ◯

C   It allows the metalworker to toughen the metal so that it will cut other metals   ◯

D   It allows the metalworker to change the shape of the metal   ◯

Metals and their Properties

Hardening

1 Explain how you would harden a piece of steel.

....

....

....

2 At what stage of hardness is a piece of steel after it has been heated to red heat? Tick the correct option.

A It depends on the type of steel ◯

B Minimum hardness ◯

C Medium hardness ◯

D Maximum hardness ◯

Tempering

3 Circle the correct options in the following sentences.

a) Steel that will not wear away, but is brittle, is **tempered / hardened**.

b) Steel that is hard, but not brittle, is **tempered / hardened**.

4 Explain why you would need to temper a piece of steel that had been hardened.

....

....

....

5 When tempering, what temperature would you heat the metal to if you wanted to use it for making taps, dies and punches? Tick the correct option.

A 230°C ◯   **B** 235°C ◯

C 240°C ◯   **D** 250°C ◯

6 When tempering, what colour would you heat the metal to if you wanted to use it for making cold chisels and saws? Tick the correct option.

A Brown ◯   **B** Brown / purple ◯

C Purple ◯   **D** Blue ◯

Types of Ferrous Metals

1 Complete the table below.

Metal	Description	Uses
a)	An alloy of iron with typically 18% chromium and 8% nickel. Very resistant to wear and corrosion and doesn't rust.	**b)** ....
Mild steel	**c)**	Nuts and bolts, furniture frames, gates, girders.
d)	Also known as 'medium' or 'high carbon' steel. Up to 1.5% carbon content. Strong and very hard.	Hand tools, e.g. chisels, screwdrivers, hammers, saws, garden tools, springs.
e)	Re-melted pig iron with some small quantities of other metals. 93% iron with 4% carbon is typical. Very strong in compression, but brittle.	**f)** ....
High speed steel	Contains a high content of tungsten, chromium and vanadium. Brittle but resistant to wear.	**g)** ....

2 Match the uses **A, B, C** and **D** with the ferrous metals **1–4** in the table. Enter the appropriate number in the boxes provided.

	Ferrous Metal
1	Cast iron
2	Stainless steel
3	Mild steel
4	High speed steel

A An outdoor table ◯

B A drill bit ◯

C A car brake drum ◯

D A car body ◯

3 Which of the following properties would a designer be looking for if they chose stainless steel for a cutlery project? Tick the **two** correct options.

A It has an interesting yellow / gold colour ◯

B It's much cheaper than mild steel ◯

C It's unlikely to rust or corrode ◯

D It doesn't taste or taint the food ◯

4 Why is mild steel often painted?

....

Non-ferrous Metals

1 Complete the table below.

Metal	Description	Uses
a) _____	Light grey in colour. Lightweight and anodised to protect the surface and to colour it.	**b)** _____
Lead	**c)** _____	Car battery cells, weather proofing, plumber's solder.
d) _____	Bright silver, ductile and malleable, resistant to corrosion.	Coating on food cans.
Copper	**e)** _____	Plumbing and electrical components, domed roofs.

2 Match the properties **A, B** and **C** with the metals **1–3** in the table. Enter the appropriate number in the boxes provided.

	Metal
1	Zinc
2	Gold
3	Silver

A Very ductile, malleable and not affected by oxidation ◯

B Very weak and extremely resistant to corrosion ◯

C Very ductile and malleable, but does tarnish ◯

3 Which of the following properties would a designer be looking for if they chose copper for a project? Tick the **three** correct options.

A It has a beautiful deep red-brown colour ◯

B It's easy to work and is malleable ◯

C It's much cheaper than steel ◯

D It's unlikely to tarnish ◯

E It's easy to solder ◯

Types of Alloys

1 (Circle) the correct options in the following sentences.

   a) **Brass / Duralumin** is an alloy of copper and zinc.

   b) **Brass / Duralumin** is an alloy of copper and aluminium.

2 Complete the table below.

Material	Properties	Uses
Pewter	**a)**	Decorative metal work and plumbing accessories.
Casting alloy (LM4)	Mainly aluminium with 3% copper and 5% silicon.	**b)**
c)	An aluminium alloy that is almost as strong as steel but 30% of the weight. Made up of aluminium, 4% copper, 1% manganese and 1% magnesium.	Aircraft bodies, cars and door handles.
Guilding metal	**d)**	**e)**

3 What is the main metal in casting alloy? Tick the correct option.

   A Brass ⬚

   B Gold ⬚

   C Aluminium ⬚

   D Pewter ⬚

4 Give two reasons why a designer might choose to use an alloy rather than a pure metal.

   a)

   b)

Marking and Joining Metals

Measuring Lengths and Angles, and Marking the Surface

1 Match the uses **A, B, C, D** and **E** with the marking out tools **1–5** in the table. Enter the appropriate number in the boxes provided.

A   Used to mark centre points and lines to be cut or filed ◯

B   Used to mark the surface of the metal ◯

C   An adjustable angle marker that can be set to any angle ◯

D   Used to mark lines at exactly 90° from the edge of the material ◯

E   Used to mark off equal divisions or make curves ◯

F   Used to measure lengths and to set tools ◯

	Marking Out Tool
1	Engineering Square
2	Sliding bevel
3	Dot punch
4	Divider
5	Scriber
6	Steel rule

2 Why should marking blue be used when marking out metals?

3 Which of the following tools is suitable for marking parallel lines on metal? Tick the **two** correct options.

A   Divider ◯

B   Odd-leg calipers ◯

C   Scriber ◯

D   Marking gauge ◯

E   Surface gauge ◯

4 Circle the correct words in the following sentences.

a) A **dot / centre** punch has a point ground to 90° and is used to mark out drilling centres.

b) A **dot / centre** punch has a point ground to 60° and is used to mark out lines to be filed.

Joining Metals

5 Circle the correct options in the following sentences.

The most common methods for joining metals are welding, **flexible / soft** soldering and hard soldering.

When soldering, the **parent / strongest** metals don't melt. The surface is cleaned with **glue / flux** and heat is then applied using a **gas torch / bunsen burner**. The solder is applied and melts and, if the surface is **clean / rough**, it will 'run' between the two parent metals.

Joining Metals

Welding

1 What do the following acronyms stand for?

   a) MIG: ....

   b) TIG: ....

2 Describe what happens in MIG welding.

....

....

....

3 In what situation would you use a gas welder?

....

4 What kind of metals are joined by TIG welding?

....

5 Circle the correct options in the following sentences.

   a) When welding you must always wear **a dark visor / goggles** to protect your eyes.

   b) When soft soldering you must always wear **a dark visor / goggles** to protect your eyes.

Soldering

6 What is the difference between hard soldering and soft soldering?

....

....

7 Give a description of the following words.

   a) Spelter

....

   b) Blowtorch

....

Joining Metals

Nuts and Bolts

1 Match the joining methods **A, B, C** and **D** with the bolt/nut head types **1–4**. Enter the appropriate number in the boxes provided.

	Bolt/Nut Head Types	Picture
1	Hexagonal head	
2	Wing nut	
3	Slotted head	
4	Hexagonal socket head	

A Screwdriver ⃝

B Allen key ⃝

C Fingers ⃝

D Spanner ⃝

2 Choose the correct words from the options given to complete the following sentences.

nut   **vibrating**   **surface**   **machine**   **dismantled**   **sprung**   **used**

different   **protect**

Nuts and bolts can be .... for repair or maintenance. They also allow

.... materials to be joined together. A washer is usually used under the

.... to spread the pressure and .... the surface. This might

be a plain ring or .... to keep the nut from .... loose.

3 Match the bolt heads **A, B** and **C** with the uses **1–3** in the table.
Enter the appropriate number in the boxes provided.

A Cheese head ⃝

B Countersunk head ⃝

C Hexagonal head ⃝

	Uses
1	Will sit level with the surface
2	Tightened with a spanner
3	Best to be used on thin metals

4 What does the abbreviated description 'M12 x 25 Hex steel bolt' mean?

....

5 Circle the correct options in the following sentences.

a) A **pop/round head** rivet is the best method for riveting a tube onto a flat or plastic sheet.

b) A **pop/round head** rivet is the best method for riveting two flat plates together.

Cutting Metals

Shearing, Bending and Pressing

1 Match the descriptions **A**, **B** and **C** with the processes **1–3** in the table. Enter the appropriate number in the boxes provided.

A Sheet metal is stamped cold using hydraulic rams that create massive pressure ◯

B Sheet metal is usually cut with heavy-duty scissors ◯

C Sheet metal can be shaped in several ways with folding bars being a common method ◯

	Processes
1	Shearing
2	Bending
3	Pressing

Drilling and Chiselling Metals

2 Which of the following types of steel are suitable for making drill bits for cutting metals? Tick the **two** correct options.

A Carbon steel ◯   **B** Tool steel ◯

C High speed steel ◯   **D** Stainless steel ◯

E Tempered steel ◯

3 Describe safety checks that you would make before using a drilling machine.

a) ....

b) ....

4 Choose the correct words from the options given to complete the following sentences.

> **tool steel**   **mild steel**   **tempered**   **soft**   **hard**   **away**
>
> **goggles**   **towards**   **vice**

Cold chisels are made from ...., which is hardened and ....

at the cutting edge. The other end of the chisel is .... to enable it to withstand

hammer blows. The chisel should only be used pointing .... from the body and

.... must always be worn.

5 Which tool would you use to cut a hole 30mm in diameter in copper sheet? Tick the correct option.

A 30mm twist drill ◯   **B** 30mm forstner bit ◯

C 30mm tank cutter ◯   **D** 30mm auger ◯   ◻

Cutting Metals

Screws

1 What size must the drilled hole be, which the tap goes into, when tapping a piece of steel?

    A The same size as the finished thread ◯

    B Larger than the finished thread ◯

    C Smaller than the finished thread ◯

    D It doesn't matter what size the hole is ◯

2 Circle the correct options in the following sentences.

    a) The thread around the outside of a piece of bar is called the **male / female** thread.

    b) The thread around the inside of a hole in a piece of bar is called the **male / female** thread.

3 Complete the table below.

Tool	Process	Holder	Description
a) _____	**b)** _____	Tap holder	**c)** _____ _____
Split die	Threading	**d)** _____	**e)** _____ _____

4 Explain what a tap is.

_____

_____

Thread Cutting

5 Circle the correct options in the following sentences.

Threads can be cut with a **saw / lathe**.

In industry, many threads are **rolled / pressed**. Hard-threaded rollers **twist / rotate** the material and press it into **shape / a mould**.

This is a form of **cold / drop / hot** forging.

Cutting Metals

Hand and Drop Forging

1 Choose the correct words from the options given to complete the following sentences.

| softens | grain | reformed | strong | crystals |
| forging | anvil | hardens | weaker |

Steel can be heated until it _____. By applying force from a hammer or a press, the

metal can be _____. This process is known as _____. Shaping by

forging rather than cutting ensures that the _____ of the metal isn't interrupted.

Forged components are very _____.

Traditionally, forging is done by the blacksmith using a hearth to heat the iron or steel and an

_____ to withstand the hammer blows.

2 Sketch the process of drop forging and explain what happens.

3 What is the name given to the cold forging process used to stamp out coins? Tick the correct option.

A Money making ◯

B Coining ◯

C Stamping ◯

D Coin stamping ◯

Cutting Metals

Sawing and Hand Saws

1 Match the uses **A, B** and **C** with the saws **1–3** in the table.
Enter the appropriate number in the boxes provided.

	Saw
1	Hacksaw
2	Junior hacksaw
3	Piercing saw

A   Used to cut out fine detail in decorative sheet metalwork   ◯

B   Used to reduce large pieces of metal to the right size for working   ◯

C   Used to reduce small pieces of metal to the right size for working   ◯

2 Choose the correct words from the options given to complete the following sentences.

friction   backward   three   triangular   twisted
four   forward   waved   frame

Sawing is one of the oldest methods of cutting materials. Teeth are _____ and

shaped so that they remove a small amount of material on the _____ stroke.

The blade is _____ to make a cut wider than the blade to reduce

_____ .

As a general guide, _____ teeth should be on the material at any time. Metal cutting

saws have small teeth on blades supported in a _____ .

3 Explain how you would cut out a shape from a piece of brass sheet that is 1mm thick.

_____

_____

_____

Machine Saws

4 What kind of motion does a powered hacksaw use? Tick the correct option.

A   Up and down   ◯

B   Rotating   ◯

C   Forwards and backwards   ◯

D   Circling   ◯

Pattern and Die Casting

1 Circle the correct options in the following sentences.

In its simplest form, casting involves **cooling /pouring** metal that has been heated and **melted /cooked** into a **mould /former**. Any **wood /waste** material can be **frozen /re-melted** and used again. **Sand /soil** casting is used to shape metals such as cast iron, aluminium and brass.

2 Number the following stages of the pattern casting process **1–8** to put them into the correct order.

A One of the boxes has two tapered holes made by sprues.

B The space left is filled with molten metal.

C Oil-bound sand is used to fill each box.

D The pattern is made in two halves and attached to a board.

E The pattern is removed carefully.

F The pattern is sandwiched between open boxes called a cope and drag.

G The cope and drag are put back together.

H A pattern is made from a timber such as MDF or Jelutong.

3 Label each part of the diagram below

b)

c)

a)

d)

g)

e)

f)

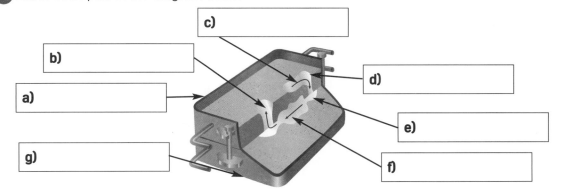

4 Match the uses **A, B, C** and **D** with the casting methods **1–4** in the table. Enter the appropriate number in the boxes provided.

A Using wax as a pattern that is melted before the silver or gold is cast

B Using a pattern made from timber. The pattern is removed and the space left is filled with molten metal

C A form of moulding used to manufacture large quantities of metal products

D Using a pattern made from polystyrene foam. Molten metal is poured into the mould

	Casting Method
1	Lost pattern casting
2	Split pattern casting
3	Lost wax casting
4	Die casting

Metal Surface Finishes

Files and Abrasive Materials

1 The table contains the names of four tools that can be used for filing.
Match the uses **A, B, C** and **D** with the tools **1–4** in the table.
Enter the appropriate number in the boxes provided.

	Tool
1	Bastard cut hand file
2	Smooth cut hand file
3	Second cut half round file
4	Second cut round file

A Used to remove material from the inside of a hole ◯

B Used to remove material quickly from a flat surface ◯

C Used to remove material from inside a curve ◯

D Used to finish a flat surface ◯

2 Choose the correct words from the options given to complete the following sentences.

steels   pressing and dragging   soft   pushing and pulling
brittle   teeth   mild steel   high carbon steel   hardened

Files are used to smooth and shape the surface of metals and hard plastics by ....

the hundreds of small .... on the file across the material. They are made from

.... and should be treated with care because they are ....

and can snap if dropped or abused. Files are made from .... steel, so they'll cut

other metals, even other ....

3 Draw a clear sketch to show the difference between cross filing and draw filing.

4 What materials are commonly used as abrasives for metal finishing? Tick the **two** correct options.

A Emery ◯   **B** Sand ◯   **C** Silicon carbide ◯   **D** Carborundum ◯

5 What materials are the abrasives for metal finishing glued onto? Tick the **two** correct options.

A Paper ◯   **B** Cardboard ◯   **C** Wood ◯   **D** Cloth ◯

6 What is the name of the sanding machines designed for abrading metals? Tick the correct option.

A Sanding machines ◯   **B** Emery machines ◯

C Linishers ◯   **D** Abraders ◯

Metal Surface Finishes

Polishing Metals

1 Choose the correct words from the options given to complete the following sentences.

buffing   **cutting**   **abrasive**   **liquid**   **solid wax**   **soft**

Metal polish is always slightly _____ as it relies on cutting away the surface of the

metal until it's very smooth. Metal polishes can be in _____ form (applied with a

cloth) or a _____ bar that is applied to a _____ wheel.

2 Which of the following metals is self-finished? Tick the correct option.

A Stainless steel ◯   **B** Steel ◯   **C** Copper ◯   **D** Silver ◯

Coatings

3 Choose the correct words from the options given to complete the following sentences.

water   **air**   **polythene**   **oven**   **thermoplastic**   **solid**
1000°C   **plastic**   **liquid**   **180°C**

_____ is the most common _____ powder, which is used for

plastic dip-coating. _____ is blown through the powder to make it behave like a

_____. Metal, pre-heated to _____, is dipped in the fluidised

powder and returned to the _____ where it melts to form a smooth finish.

4 Which of the following metals are dip coated? Tick the correct option.

A Stainless steel ◯   **B** Steel ◯   **C** Brass ◯   **D** Gold ◯

Anodising, Plating and Galvanising

5 The table contains the names of three types of metal finish.

Match descriptions **A**, **B** and **C** with the finishes **1–3** in the table.
Enter the appropriate number in the boxes provided.

	Finish
1	Plating
2	Anodising
3	Galvanising

A A process used on aluminium to provide a durable finish ◯

B A thin layer of metal on the surface provides a durable finish ◯

C A metal (usually mild steel) dipped into a bath of molten zinc ◯

Plastics

Polymerisation

1 Choose the correct words from the options given to complete the following sentences.

polymerisation   properties   links   synthetic   least

monomers   polymers   chains

There are many different plastics and they all have different _____.

_____ plastics are manufactured using a process known as

_____. This occurs when _____ join together to form long

_____ of molecules called polymers.

2 What kind of plastic are amber and latex? Tick the correct option.

A Synthetic ⬭

B Natural ⬭

C Man-made ⬭

D Thermoplastics ⬭

Types of Plastics

3 Circle the correct options in the following sentences.

a) Plastics that can be re-softened by heating are **thermosetting plastics / thermoplastics**.

b) Plastics that can't be re-softened by heating are **thermosetting plastics / thermoplastics**.

4 A plastic will harden when it's cooled, but can be reshaped if heated up again. What is this process called? Tick the correct option.

A Posting ⬭   **B** Post forming ⬭

C Forming later ⬭   **D** Bending ⬭

5 Match the descriptions **A, B, C** and **D** with the properties **1–4** in the table. Enter the appropriate number in the boxes provided.

A Different plastics differ greatly in colour ⬭

B Plastics vary from weak to very strong ⬭

C Some plastics are much easier to work with than others ⬭

D Some plastics can be recovered at 'end of life' ⬭

	Properties
1	Workability
2	Can be recycled
3	Appearance
4	Structural strength

Thermoplastics

1 What do the following acronyms stand for?

a) HDPE: ....

b) PP: ....

c) HIPS: ....

d) PVC: ....

2 Complete the table below.

Plastic	Description	Uses
Polythene (high density)	**a)**	**b)** ....
Nylon	Hard material with good resistance to wear and tear	**c)** ....
Perspex (Acrylic)	**d)**	Display signs, baths, roof lights and machine guards
High impact polystyrene	Light but strong plastic. Widely available in sheet form. Softens at about 95°C	**e)** ....
PVC	Stiff and hard-wearing. A plasticiser can be added to create a softer, more rubbery material	**f)** ....

3 What is low-density polythene used for? Tick the **two** correct options.

A Milk crates ⬜   **B** Carrier bags ⬜

C Windows ⬜   **D** 'Squeezy' detergent bottles ⬜

4 What property of nylon makes it suitable to use for making clothing? Tick the correct option.

A It doesn't rust ⬜   **B** It's resistant to wear and tear ⬜

C It's a weak fabric ⬜   **D** It's very strong ⬜

Plastics

1 Complete the table below.

Plastic	Description	Uses
Phenol formaldehyde	Hard, brittle plastic. Dark colour with a glossy finish. Heat resistant	a)
b)	c)	Laminated to form Glass Reinforced Plastic (GRP)
d)	Heat-resistant polymer	Tableware, electrical installations, decorative laminates and worktops

2 What do the following acronyms stand for?

a) MF:

b) PR:

c) ER:

3 Circle the correct options in the following sentences.

a) **Bakelite / GRP / Urea formaldehyde** is a thermosetting composite plastic used to make car bodies and boats.

b) **Bakelite / GRP / Urea formaldehyde** is a thermosetting plastic used to make handles for kettles, irons and saucepans.

c) **Bakelite / GRP / Urea formaldehyde** is a thermosetting plastic used to make electrical switches and electrical fittings.

4 How is epoxy resin prepared for use? Tick the correct option.

A By being mixed with water ◯

B By squeezing it out of a tube ◯

C By heating it in a small pot ◯

D By mixing a resin and a hardener ◯

Marking Out Plastics

Measuring Lengths and Angles

1 Which of the following tools is suitable for marking lines at right angles to a side on plastic? Tick the correct option.

A Surface gauge ◯   **B** Tri square ◯

C Sliding bevel ◯   **D** Marking gauge ◯

2 Which of the following tools is suitable for marking lines at 37° to a side on plastic? Tick the correct option.

A Surface gauge ◯   **B** Tri square ◯

C Sliding bevel ◯   **D** Marking gauge ◯

Marking the Surface

3 Choose the correct words from the options given to complete the following sentences.

pencil   protective   scriber   scratched   polished

decorative   removed

When marking out plastics, it's sensible to leave the .... covering on the surface

for as long as possible. This helps to prevent the plastic from being ....

Mark out on this covering using a .... or a fine-liner pen. The covering can be

.... when all other processes have finished.

4 Match the uses **A, B, C** and **D** with the marking out tools **1–3** in the table. Enter the appropriate number in the boxes provided.

	Tool
1	Compass
2	Card stencil
3	Centre punch

A Used to mark out circles or arcs ◯

B Used for marking out curved shapes onto any material ◯

C Used for marking the centre of holes for drilling into plastic ◯

5 How would you prevent the point of a compass from sliding on a plastic surface without damaging the plastic? Tick the correct option.

A Use a dot punch to mark the centre ◯

B Put a piece of masking tape at the centre of the circle ◯

C Drill a hole to mark the centre ◯

D Use a protective covering ◯

Moulding Plastics

1 Complete the table below.

Process	Description	Uses
Line bending	a) _____	b) _____
c) _____	The pressure from a close-fitting yoke will hold the plastic until it has hardened	d) _____
Vacuum forming	e) _____	Any tapered three-dimensional shape

2 Which would be the most suitable plastic to use for vacuum forming? Tick the correct option.

   A Foamed PVC ◯   **B** Epoxy resin ◯

   C High impact polystyrene ◯   **D** Nylon ◯

3 Which would be the most suitable plastic to use for yoke forming? Tick the correct option.

   A Foamed PVC ◯   **B** Epoxy resin ◯

   C High impact polystyrene ◯   **D** Nylon ◯

4 Which would be the most suitable material to use for making a former for line bending at 90°? Tick the correct option.

   A Walnut ◯   **B** Mild steel ◯   **C** Polystyrene ◯   **D** MDF ◯

Injection Moulding

5 Number the following injection moulding processes **1–4** to put them into the correct order.

   A Pressure is maintained on the mould, until it has cooled enough to be opened. ◯

   B Plastic powder or granules are fed from the hopper into a hollow steel barrel. ◯

   C Once enough melted plastic has collected, the hydraulic system forces the plastic into the mould. ◯

   D The heaters melt the plastic as the screw moves it along towards the mould. ◯

Injection Moulding (Cont.)

1 What are the typical materials used in injection moulding? Tick the **two** correct options.

A Polythene and polystyrene ☐

B Expanded polystyrene and polyurethane ☐

C Melamine and urea formaldehyde ☐

D Polypropylene and nylon ☐

2 How could injection moulding be carried out in a school workshop? Tick the correct option.

A By using a funnel to guide the molten plastic into the cavity ☐

B By using a steel bar to melt the plastic ☐

C By using a vacuum forming machine ☐

D By using a hot glue gun and a simple mould made from two pieces of steel with a cavity between them ☐

Extrusion

3 Circle the correct words in the following sentences.

Plastic **granules / sheets** are fed from the **hopper / die** by the rotating screw. They are heated as they are fed through to a **former / mould**.

The difference between the injection moulding process and the extrusion process is that the softened plastic is forced through a **screw / die** in a **continuous / broken** stream, to create long tube or sectional extrusions.

The extrusions are then passed through a **heated / cooling** chamber and cut to the required length.

4 What are the typical materials used in extrusion? Tick the correct option.

A Polythene, PVC and nylon ☐

B Expanded polystyrene and polyurethane ☐

C Melamine and urea formaldehyde ☐

D Polypropylene and polyester ☐

Moulding Plastics

Blow Moulding

1 Number the following processes **1–4** to put them into the correct order to explain the blow moulding process.

    A The mould is cooled and then opened to remove the product. ◯

    B The expanded air forces plastic to the sides of the mould. ◯

    C Air is blown into an extruded section of tube where it expands. ◯

    D The plastic is heated. ◯

2 Choose the correct words from the options given to complete the following sentences.

    split   **polythene**   **air**   **cooling**   **water**   **extrusion**   **vacuum**

Common materials used for blow moulding are PVC, _____ and polypropylene.

This process is similar to the _____ process, apart from the use of an

_____ supply and a _____ mould instead of the

_____ chamber.

Rotational Moulding

3 Number the following processes **1–5** to put them into the correct order to explain the rotational moulding process.

    A The mould splits apart to put plastic inside. ◯

    B On cooling, the mould is opened up and the product is ejected. ◯

    C Heat is applied while the mould is rotated. ◯

    D The plastic is poured into the mould. ◯

    E Plastic is thrown outwards to the inner surface of the mould. ◯

Compression Moulding

4 Which description best describes compression moulding? Tick the correct option.

    A A sheet of plastic sucked into a mould and held until cool ◯

    B A large force used to squash a cube of polymer into a heated mould ◯

    C A piece of plastic moulded over a former ◯

    D A large force used to compress glass fibres until they melt ◯

Cutting Plastics

Sawing

1 What is the ideal number of teeth per inch for a saw blade used for cutting plastic? Tick the correct option.

A 5 TPI ◯   **B** 10 TPI ◯

C 20 TPI ◯   **D** 30 TPI ◯

2 Why is it important to choose the correct number of teeth per inch for a saw blade?

3 Match the plastic cutting processes **A**, **B** and **C** with the tools **1–3** in the table. Enter the appropriate number in the boxes provided.

A Used for sawing curves ◯

B Used for sawing straight lines ◯

C Used for sawing straight lines where accuracy is needed ◯

Tool	
1	Hacksaw
2	Junior hacksaw
3	Coping saw

4 How can you prevent the blade from sticking when sawing plastic on a machine jigsaw? Tick the correct option.

A Saw very slowly ◯

B Put a piece of masking tape on the surface ◯

C Use a very coarse blade ◯

D Use a very fine blade ◯

Drilling and Hand Planing

5 Which tools could you use to make a 30mm diameter hole in a 3mm thick piece of acrylic? Tick the **two** correct options.

A A twist drill ◯   **B** A hole saw ◯

C A junior hacksaw ◯   **D** A tank cutter ◯

6 Which tools could you use to finish the edge of a 6mm thick piece of acrylic? Tick the **two** correct options.

A A steel rule ◯   **B** A rasp ◯

C A bevel-edged chisel ◯   **D** A block plane ◯

Joining and Finishing Plastics

Nuts and Bolts

1 Explain what the following items are and how they are used.

a) Bolt: ....

b) Nut: ....

c) Washer: ....

d) Spring washer: ....

2 Choose the correct words from the options given to complete the following sentences.

temporary	tap and die	materials	permanent
female	screw	injection	bolt

Nuts and bolts are .... fastenings that can join plastics together or to other

.... Threads are sometimes cut into one piece of the plastic and a machine

.... is then used to hold plastic components together. Plastic threads are usually

.... moulded, rather than being cut with a ....

Adhesives and Solvent Cement

3 Which adhesives could you use to glue two pieces of 6mm thick acrylic together? Tick the **two** correct options.

A Solvents (tensol) ◯   B PVA ◯

C Epoxy resin (araldite) ◯   D Cascamite ◯

4 In what situation might you use a glue gun when working with plastics? Tick the **two** correct options.

A When making a box ◯   B When prototyping ◯

C As a permanent join ◯   D For quick modelling ◯

5 What safety precautions should be taken when using solvents to glue plastics? Tick the **three** correct options.

A Using adequate ventilation because dangerous fumes are given off ◯

B Wearing latex gloves because solvents are toxic ◯

C Wearing goggles to protect your eyes from the solvent spray ◯

D Wearing ear protection because of the loud noise created ◯

Plastics and Smart Materials

Self-finishing and Polishing Plastics

1 What is meant by the term 'self-finished'?

2 Why don't the surfaces of sheet plastics need to be finished unless they've been damaged?

3 Number the following stages **1–4** to put them into the correct order to explain how a plastic is finished.

A Different grades of wet and dry paper are then
moistened with water and used to make the edge smooth. ◯

B The edge is polished to a high shine using 'brasso'. ◯

C A smooth file can be drawn along the edge of the plastic. ◯

D The edge is polished on a buffing wheel. ◯

4 What is the name for the final type of filing that can be used on a plastic edge? Tick the correct option.

A Cross filing ◯ **B** Draw filing ◯ **C** Long filing ◯ **D** Short filing ◯

New Materials and Smart Alloys

5 Choose the correct words from the options given to complete the following sentences.

bent   **remember**   **heated**   **shape memory alloy**   **returns**   **cooled**   **hit**

A smart alloy is a material that can .... its original shape. Another name for a

smart alloy is a .... Examples of this type of alloy are nickel-titanium, copper-zinc-

aluminium and copper-aluminium-nickel. When the alloy is .... or twisted, it keeps

its new shape until it's .... When the temperature is raised to a certain level, the

alloy .... to its original shape.

6 What happens to a smart wire when a small electric current is passed through it? Tick the correct option.

A It will heat up ◯   **B** It will expand in length ◯

C It will change colour ◯   **D** It will shrink in length ◯

7 Give one application where a designer could use a smart wire.

◯

Smart and Composite Materials

Smart Steel and Plastics

1 What happens when smart steels are stressed? Tick the correct option.

A They become magnetic ⬭   **B** They cool down ⬭

C They expand ⬭   **D** They contract ⬭

2 What can smart steels be used for? _____

3 Circle the correct options from the following sentences.

Polymorph is a tough **metal / polymer** (plastic) that **hardens / softens** and becomes easy to mould at only **62°C / 40°C**. This means that it can be softened with **cold / hot** water or a hairdryer and moulded into shape by hand. It hardens to a very stiff plastic.

Smart Colours and Other Smart Materials

4 What happens to smart colours when they're heated? Tick the correct option.

A They glow in the dark ⬭   **B** They change shape ⬭

C They are radioactive ⬭   **D** They change colour above 27°C ⬭

5 Circle the correct options in the following sentences.

Smart grease is a very **smooth / sticky** and viscous gel that can be used to **control / stop** the movement of mechanisms. For example, on a rubber band driven toy it can **limit / regulate** the speed at which the **potential / kinetic** energy is released.

Composites

6 Choose the correct words from the options given to complete the following sentences.

a) Resin that has been reinforced by the addition of strands of spun glass fibres is known as reinforced **polyester / concrete.**

b) Cement mixed with water, sand and aggregate, which has been reinforced by the addition of steel bars, is known as reinforced **polyester / concrete.**

7 What is reinforced concrete used for? Tick the **two** correct options.

A Building cars ⬭   **B** Construction of bridges ⬭

C Construction of buildings ⬭   **D** Construction of boat hulls ⬭

8 What is GRP used for? Tick the **two** correct options.

A Building car bodies ⬭   **B** Construction of bridges ⬭

C Construction of buildings ⬭   **D** Construction of boat hulls ⬭

Smart and Composite Materials

Other Composites

1 (Circle) the correct words in the following sentences.

a) Kevlar / Tufnol is a lightweight, high-pressure laminate that has good strength and electrical insulating properties and is used in marine environments.

b) Kevlar / Tufnol is a cord that is laminated with plastics to give exceptional strength and resistance to strain and is used for cut-resistant gloves.

2 What is Kevlar used for? Tick the **two** correct options.

A Protective equipment ◯		**B** Marine environments	◯
C Body armour ◯		**D** Situations requiring very long life outdoors	◯

3 What is Tufnol used for? Tick the **two** correct options.

A Protective equipment, e.g. cut-resistant gloves ◯

B Marine environments ◯

C Body armour ◯

D Outdoor situations requiring a very long life ◯

4 Choose the correct words from the options given to complete the following sentences.

composite   **bends**   **thermostats**   **expansion**

pressure   **temperature**   **contraction**

A bi-metallic strip is a _____ of two metals with different rates of

_____ . When the _____ changes, the metal with the greater rate

of expansion _____ round the other. They are used for simple temperature sensing

devices, e.g. _____ in heating systems.

Nano Materials

5 What does the term 'nano' mean in the name 'nano materials'? Tick the correct option.

A Very large, more than 50nm ◯		**B** Very small, less than 50nm	◯
C Protection ◯		**D** Particle	◯

6 What can a nano material be used for? Tick the **three** correct options.

A To make self-cleaning glass ◯		**B** As quick dissolving medicines	◯
C In paint as a flame retarder ◯		**D** To reinforce concrete	◯

Milling, Routing and Turning

Milling and Routing

1 Choose the correct words from the options given to complete the following sentences.

| **milling** | **multi-toothed** | **bladed** | **routing** | **template** |

Milling and routing machines use a revolving _____ cutter. Cutting metals and plastics

is known as _____. Cutting timber is known as _____.

Shapes can be cut manually using a powered router. This can follow a _____ in

order to shape the edge of a timber board.

2 Which of the following statements describe possible uses for a hand-held router? Tick the **three** correct options.

A Making round legs for a stool ◯

B Making a moulded edge around a table top ◯

C Cutting dovetail joints ◯

D Making a half-lap joint ◯

CNC Milling

3 Choose the correct words from the options given to complete the following sentences.

| **computer aided design** | **manually** | **computer numerical control** |
| **stepper motor** | **computer aided manufacture** | **mechanically** |

Traditional milling machines can be controlled by moving the blade through each axis _____.

By moving each axis with a _____, very accurate movements can be controlled using

_____. This is one of the most common forms of _____.

Centre Lathes

4 Circle the correct option in the following sentence.

Turning metals and plastics on a centre lathe involves holding the work in a chuck and rotating the work **away from / towards** the cutter.

5 What important safety precautions should be taken when turning materials on a lathe? Tick the **three** correct options.

A Wear a visor ◯

B Wear latex gloves ◯

C Wear a dust mask ◯

D Switch on the dust extractor ◯

© Lonsdale

Wood-turning Lathe

1 Name three different types of wood-turning chisel.

a) _____

b) _____

c) _____

2 Circle the correct options in the following sentences.

a) When using a wood-turning lathe, the tool is **rested on a support and is guided by hand / held in a tool post and guided by turning a wheel.**

b) When using a centre lathe, the tool is **rested on a support and is guided by hand / held in a tool post and guided by turning a wheel.**

3 In which ways can work be held securely when turning on a lathe? Tick the **two** correct options.

A The work can be held between centres ⬭

B The work can be held by using a cramp ⬭

C The work can be held in a machine vice ⬭

D The work can be screwed onto a faceplate ⬭

CNC Turning

4 What piece of machinery controls both the work and cutting tools on a CNC centre lathe? Tick the correct option.

A Hacksaw blade ⬭

B Powered router ⬭

C Stepper motor ⬭

D Tank cutter ⬭

5 What kind of items are CNC lathes usually used to turn? Tick the correct option.

A Large quantities of identical pieces ⬭

B Small quantities of individual pieces ⬭

C Large quantities of different shaped pieces ⬭

D Small quantities of circular pieces ⬭

Levers

1 **a)** What is name of the movement that only moves in one direction? Tick the correct option.

A Linear ⬭

B Reciprocating ⬭

C Rotary ⬭

D Oscillating ⬭

b) Give one example of a product that uses this type of motion.

_____

2 **a)** What is name of the movement that swings in alternate directions? Tick the correct option.

A Linear ⬭

B Reciprocating ⬭

C Rotary ⬭

D Oscillating ⬭

b) Give one example of a product that uses this type of motion.

_____

3 Draw an arrow showing reciprocating movement.

Levers 1 – Basic Principles

4 Choose the correct words from the options given to complete the following sentences.

      fulcrum   **pivots**   **balances**   **load**   **effort**   **work**

A lever is a simple device, consisting of a rigid bar, which _____ about a fixed point,

called a _____ .

A _____ is applied at one end of a 'rigid bar'. The bar is placed centrally on top

of the pivot point. At the other end of the bar a force is applied (called the _____).

This results in a single lever movement about the pivot point.

First Class Levers

1 Choose the correct words from the options given to complete the following sentences.

multipliers   **smaller**   **fulcrum**   **effort**

load   **mechanical advantage**   **larger**

Levers can be force _____. By altering the position of the _____,

the effort can be multiplied and a larger load can be lifted. This is called the _____.

The fulcrum is between the load and the _____, so the effort needed is less than the load.

2 Give one example of a product that uses a first class lever system. _____

Second and Third Class Levers

3 Complete the sketch to show where the fulcrum would be placed for a second class lever.

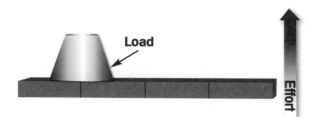

4 Give the name of one product that uses a second class lever system. _____

5 Complete the sketch to show where the fulcrum would be placed for a third class lever.

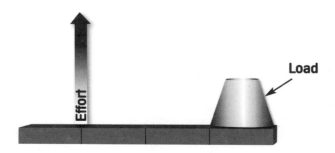

6 Which product uses a third class lever system? Tick the correct option.

A The human arm ◯   **B** A wheelbarrow ◯

C A crowbar ◯   **D** A clock pendulum ◯

Cranks and Cams

General Mechanical Movement

1 Circle the correct option in the following sentence.

Cranks and cams are relatively simple devices that convert **rotary motion to reciprocating motion /
reciprocating motion to oscillating motion.**

2 The diagram shows a cam mechanism.

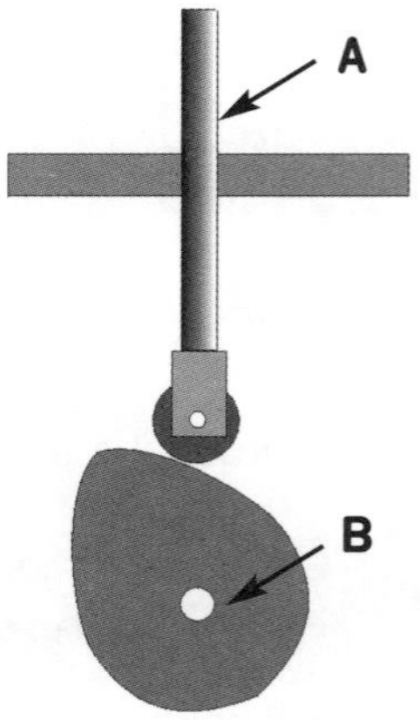

a) What is part A called? Tick the correct option.

A Follower ◯   B Guide ◯

C Cam ◯   D Crank ◯

b) What is part B called? Tick the correct option.

A Follower ◯   B Guide ◯

C Cam ◯   D Crank ◯

Cranks

3 Where could you find a crank mechanism? Tick the **three** correct options.

A The pedal mechanism of a tricycle ◯

B A car engine valve opening system ◯

C A car engine crankshaft ◯

D A toy with a part that moves as the wheels rotate ◯

Cams

4 Where could you find a cam mechanism? Tick the **two** correct options.

A The pedal mechanism of a tricycle ◯

B A car engine valve opening system ◯

C A car engine crankshaft ◯

D A toy with a part that moves as the wheels rotate ◯

5 Explain what each of the following terms mean:

a) Follower: ....

b) Guide: ....

c) Cam: ....

Springs

1 The table contains the names of four spring types.

Match pictures **A**, **B**, **C** and **D** with the springs **1–4** in the table. Enter the appropriate number in the boxes provided.

	Spring
1	Radial movement
2	Twisting
3	Extension
4	Compression

A ◯

B ◯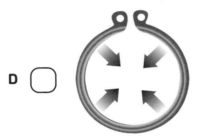

C ◯

D ◯

Linkages

2 Show, using arrows to give the direction of movement, how this linkage works.

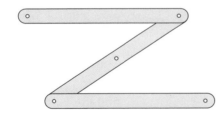

3 Show, using arrows to give the direction of movement, how this linkage works.

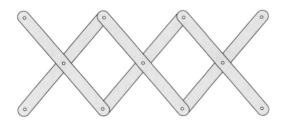

4 What are linkages often used to connect? Tick the **two** correct options.

A Gears to cranks ◯

B Cam followers to levers ◯

C Pulleys to gears ◯

D Cranks to levers ◯

Gears and Pulleys

Gears

1 (Circle) the correct options in the following sentences.

Gears are linkages for transferring **speed / motion**. Gear wheels have **cogs / teeth** around the edge, which **stick / mesh** with the teeth of another gear. Gear systems may also be **linked / fastened** to chains or belts.

2 The table contains the names of four gear systems that can be used for engineering. Match descriptions **A, B, C** and **D** with the systems **1–4** in the table. Enter the appropriate number in the boxes provided.

A Used to convert the rotary motion of a car's steering wheel into a lateral movement of the wheels ◯

B The small pinion moves the big pinion, which has twice as many teeth so rotates at half the speed ◯

C Changes motion through 90°. It gives a large reduction in speed and a high torque ◯

D Changes motion through 90°. If the gears are different sizes there will be a change in speed ◯

	Gear System
1	Bevel gears
2	Pinions
3	Worm and worm wheel
4	Rack and pinion

Chain and Sprocket, and Pulleys

3 Choose the correct words from the options given to complete the following sentences.

comfortable   **pedals**   **chain**   **sprocket**   **pinion**   **stretch**

The chain on a bicycle connects the _____ to the back wheel. As the pedal is pushed

by your feet the _____ links with the _____ and the wheel turns. Having a

set of sprockets makes it possible to pedal at a _____ speed when there are hills.

4 (Circle) the correct options in the following sentences.

a) A pulley is a wheel with a groove around it in which a **chain / belt** runs.

b) A sprocket is a wheel with teeth around it on which a **chain / belt** runs.

5 What is the best way to reverse direction in a pulley system? Tick the correct option.

A Run it more slowly ◯

B Include a gear box in the system ◯

C Put a twist in the belt ◯

D Change the belt for a chain ◯

Electrical Components

Components

1 What could a designer do to save energy when designing a circuit for a small torch? Tick the **two** correct options.

- **A** Consider using mains electricity ☐
- **B** Consider using solar panels to re-charge batteries ☐
- **C** Consider using disposable batteries ☐
- **D** Consider using a wind-up clockwork system ☐

2 Why should a designer consider using rechargeable batteries? Tick the correct option.

- **A** It costs less to buy rechargeable batteries ☐
- **B** It reduces the number of toxic by-products being put into landfill ☐
- **C** They are safer to use ☐
- **D** They give more power then disposable batteries ☐

3 Briefly explain what the function of a switch is.

....

....

4 Why would it be better to use an LED rather than a bulb as an indicator in a small circuit?

....

....

5 How can the direction of rotation be easily changed on a DC motor? Tick the correct option.

- **A** By changing over the connections to the battery ☐
- **B** By changing over the wires in the mains ☐
- **C** By using a different motor ☐
- **D** By using gears to reverse the direction ☐

Assembly

6 How can components be protected when being soldered into a circuit? Tick the correct option.

- **A** Don't solder, use a clip-in system ☐
- **B** Solder in a stream of cold air ☐
- **C** Use a low melting point solder ☐
- **D** Use a pair of pliers as a heat sink ☐

7 Give one safety precaution that you should take when soldering components.

....

☐

AQA-style Exam Questions

Section A

Context Garden Furniture

Design Brief

A company that manufactures and designs garden furniture has asked you to help them extend their range of products by producing a new design for a folding garden table that is suitable for putting food and drinks on at a party.

Question 1 is about the design specification.

1 Analyse the design brief shown above and evaluate what specific issues relating to the design should be considered when designing the folding garden table.

_____

_____

_____

_____

_____

_____

_____

_____

(6 marks)

Question 2 is about design ideas.

2 Study the information given in the design brief and your design specification.

Use this information to help you sketch five different ideas for a folding garden table that is suitable to use for putting food and drinks on at a party.

Marks will be awarded for creativity, originality and diversity.

(5 x 2 marks) = 10 marks

AQA-style Exam Questions

Question 3 is about evaluation.

3 Identify your best idea from Question 2. **Best idea:** ....

Evaluate your best idea against the original specification.

....

....

....

(3 marks)

Question 4 is about developing an idea. You are advised to spend about 15 minutes on this question.

4 Use notes and sketches to develop your chosen idea.

Show details of materials, sizes and the method(s) of construction.

Marks will be awarded for: quality of sketching *(4 marks)*; quality of notes *(2 marks)*; specific materials *(3 marks)*; important sizes *(2 marks)*; constructional details *(4 marks)*

(15 marks)

Section B

Question 5 is about tools, equipment and safety.

5 (a) Name each of the following tools.

Give specific details of a process where you would use each one.

Tool A

Name:

....

.... *(1 mark)*

Process:

....

.... *(1 mark)*

Name:

....

Tool B

.... *(1 mark)*

Process:

....

.... *(1 mark)*

Name:

....

Tool C

.... *(1 mark)*

Process:

....

.... *(1 mark)*

5 (b) Study the picture of the craft knife.

Complete the risk assessment table for the craft knife.

An example has been given.

Hazard	Precaution
The blade may slip and cut a finger.	Keep both hands away from the line of the cut.

(8 marks)

AQA-style Exam Questions

Question 6 is about making.

Two designs for a recipe-book stand are shown below. Both of them could be made in a school workshop.

Choose one of the recipe-book stands.

Recipe-book stand A

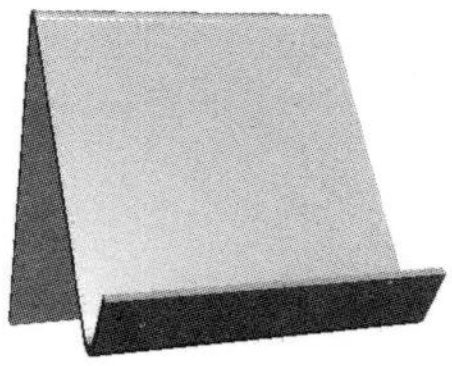

Recipe-book stand B

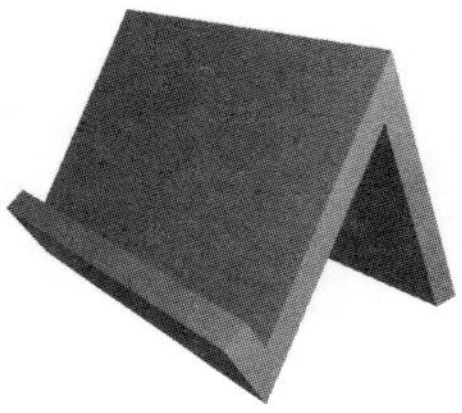

Stand chosen: ....

6 (a) Name one suitable, *specific* material you could use to make your recipe-book stand.

Give one reason for your choice.

Material:

.... *(2 marks)*

Reason:

.... *(1 mark)*

6 (b) Use notes and sketches to clearly show how you would make a batch of 10 recipe-book stands in a school workshop.

At each stage, name all the tools, equipment or software you would use.

Stage 1: Marking out **or** CAD (Computer Aided Design)

(4 marks)

Stage 2: Cutting and shaping **or** CAM (Computer Aided Manufacture)

(4 marks)

Stage 3: Bending **or** joining

(4 marks)

Stage 4: Applying the surface finish

(2 marks)

Total 17 marks

Question 7 is about materials.

7 (a) Study the products shown below.

Name one suitable, *specific* material that has been used to make each product.

Give one reason for each choice.

Product A

Material:

....

.... *(1 mark)*

Reason:

....

.... *(1 mark)*

Product B

Material:

....

.... *(1 mark)*

Reason:

....

.... *(1 mark)*

Product C

Material:

....

.... *(1 mark)*

Reason:

....

.... *(1 mark)*

7 (b) Briefly describe how plastic is obtained from oil.

(2 marks)

7 (c) Explain the sustainability issues of using oil.

(3 marks)

7 (d) i) Name a suitable **smart** material that could be used to make a prototype of a handle for a cupboard.

(1 mark)

7 (d) ii) Explain the advantages of using this smart material.

(4 marks)

OCR-style Exam Questions

Section A

1. This symbol stands for:

A wear a dust mask ☐

B beware spacemen ☐

C do not use spray guns ☐

D doctors only ☐

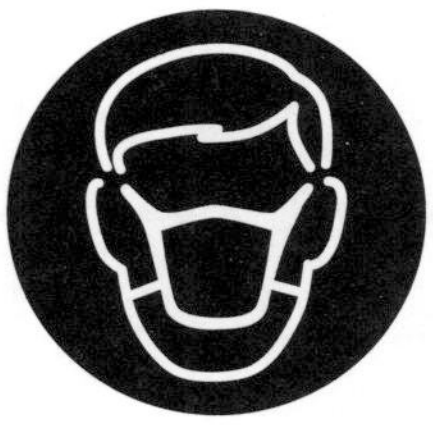

(1 mark)

2. A round red warning sign means:

A specific behaviour or action ☐

B be careful or take precautions ☐

C dangerous behaviour that you must avoid ☐

D escape routes ☐

(1 mark)

3. Which of the following is a renewable energy resource?

A wood ☐

B oil ☐

C coal ☐

D nuclear ☐

(1 mark)

4. Recyclable means that things can:

A be grown easily ☐

B be reprocessed and used as a different product ☐

C be re-used as a different product ☐

D be thrown away ☐

(1 mark)

5. One responsibility of a designer of environmentally friendly wooden products is:

A to use only natural resources ☐

B to always use recycled materials ☐

C to buy the cheapest materials ☐

D to ensure that materials come from sustainable forests ☐

(1 mark)

6. In the space below sketch the symbol that means 'wear eye protection'.

(1 mark)

7 The term **repair** means to be able to…

....

(1 mark)

8 The term **reduce** means…

....

(1 mark)

9 What does the term **inclusive design** mean?

....

(1 mark)

10 What is the name given to retailers who consider the welfare of the planet and the people who live on it?

....

(1 mark)

11 Decide whether each of the following statements is *true* or *false*.

    a) Anthropometrics is the study of human measurements.   TRUE ⬭   FALSE ⬭   *(1 mark)*

    b) A client comes up with new ideas for a design problem.   TRUE ⬭   FALSE ⬭   *(1 mark)*

    c) Manufacturers specialise in different types of production.   TRUE ⬭   FALSE ⬭   *(1 mark)*

    d) Quality control is a series of checks carried out while the product is being made.   TRUE ⬭   FALSE ⬭   *(1 mark)*

    e) Batch production means that the factory runs 24/7.   TRUE ⬭   FALSE ⬭   *(1 mark)*

Total: 15 marks

Section B

Finite resources are materials that can't be replaced once they have been used up.

A designer must think about the impact that the use of such resources will have on the environment.

12 (a) Explain how the 6 Rs will help to guide a designer.

Reduce:

....

....

(2 marks)

Recycle:

....

....

(2 marks)

Re-use:

....

....

(2 marks)

Repair:

....

....

(2 marks)

Refuse:

....

....

(2 marks)

Re-think:

....

....

(2 marks)

OCR-style Exam Questions

A designer is developing a range of environmentally friendly containers made from wood.

12 (b) Name one suitable product that could be made from wood.

....

(1 mark)

12 (c) Identify four specification points for your chosen design product.

Point 1: ....

(1 mark)

Point 2: ....

(1 mark)

Point 3: ....

(1 mark)

Point 4: ....

(1 mark)

Total 17 marks

13 (a) Use sketches and notes to show your initial ideas for your chosen product.

(6 marks)

13 (b) Use notes and sketches to develop one of your initial ideas.

(5 marks)

13 (c) (i) What method would you use to make this idea?

_____

(1 mark)

(ii) Describe four stages relevant to this technique/method.

Stage 1:

_____

(1 mark)

Stage 2:

_____

(1 mark)

Stage 3:

_____

(1 mark)

Stage 4:

_____

(1 mark)

13 (d) Name a piece of equipment that would be needed for your technique / method.

(2 marks)

13 (e) Give two safety precautions that should be taken into account when using tools and equipment.

Precaution 1:

(1 mark)

Precaution 2:

(1 mark)

Total 20 marks

1 Which of the following is an alloy?

   A Copper ◯   **B** Brass ◯

   C Gold ◯   **D** Iron ◯   *(1 mark)*

2 What type of fittings would be used for a self-assembly cupboard?

   A Dovetail joints ◯   **B** Knock-down fittings ◯

   C Door fittings ◯   **D** Halving joints ◯   *(1 mark)*

3 Which of the following joining methods requires the use of an adhesive?

   A Welding ◯   **B** Soldering ◯

   C Riveting ◯   **D** Housing joint ◯   *(1 mark)*

4 Which of the following joints requires separate components?

   A Mortice and tenon joint ◯   **B** Rivet joint ◯

   C Butt joint ◯   **D** Lap joint ◯   *(1 mark)*

5 Which of the following is **not** recyclable?

   A Concrete ◯   **B** Wood ◯

   C Steel ◯   **D** PVC ◯   *(1 mark)*

6 Which of the following is the most suitable method of joining two pieces of copper?

   A Gluing ◯   **B** Welding ◯

   C Soldering ◯   **D** Solvent welding ◯   *(1 mark)*

7 Which of the following is the correct definition of **malleability**?

   A A material's ability to regain its original shape after it has been deformed ◯

   B A material's ability to change permanently in shape without cracking or breaking ◯

   C A material's ability to be stretched and permanently deformed without breaking ◯

   D A material's ability to be easily pressed, spread and hammered into shape ◯   *(1 mark)*

8 Which of the following metals is alloyed with tin and copper to make low melting point pewter?

A Antimony ◯   B Zinc ◯

C Iron ◯   D Lead ◯   *(1 mark)*

9 Pouring molten liquids into a hollow and allowing them to cool is known as…

A Injecting ◯   B Extruding ◯

C Casting ◯   D Moulding ◯   *(1 mark)*

10 Tempering is a heat treatment process. The purpose of tempering is to…

A Make the item change into an alloy   ◯

B Increase the softness of an item   ◯

C Harden the item by heating it   ◯

D Make the item tougher by heating it up to a certain temperature and dipping it in cold water ◯

(1 mark)

Total 10 marks

11 The table below shows some tools and components.

Complete the table by giving the missing names and uses.

Tool/Component	Name	Use
	i)	Chiselling wood where an angle of less than 90° is needed, e.g. a dovetail joint.
	Spokeshave	ii)
	iii)	Holding a material still while working on it.
	iv)	Marking out parallel lines on metals.

(4 marks)

12 The photograph shows a book support made from a painted mild steel sheet and bar.

12 (a) Give two properties of mild steel that make it suitable for the book support.

Property 1:

....

....
(*2 marks*)

Property 2:

....

....
(*2 marks*)

12 (b) The surface of the book support has been painted.

Complete the flow chart to show the main stages in painting the steel.

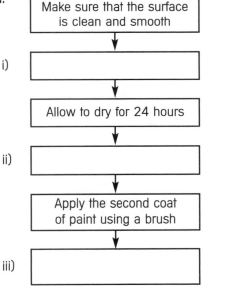

| Make sure that the surface is clean and smooth |

i) [ ]

| Allow to dry for 24 hours |

ii) [ ]

| Apply the second coat of paint using a brush |

iii) [ ]

(*6 marks*)

12 (c) Instead of using a paint finish, the hanging book support could have been dip-coated using a fluidising chamber.

Describe one advantage of dip-coating the book support.

....

....
(*2 marks*)

12 (d) Explain why the book support is successful in meeting the following specification points:

(i) Supporting the weight of the books.

....

....

(2 marks)

(ii) Stopping the books from falling over.

....

....

(2 marks)

(iii) Making it easy to see what books are on the stand.

....

....

(2 marks)

Total: 18 marks

13 You have been asked to design a trivet to hold a hot dish when it's put onto a table.

The following is the required specification for the trivet:

- It must hold one hot dish of maximum diameter 300mm
- It must have a stable base
- It must not harm the table surface it sits on
- It must protect the table surface from the hot dish
- It must be made from heat-proof materials
- It must be manufactured in a batch of 10 in a school workshop

Use sketches and brief notes to show **two** different design ideas for the trivet that meet the specification points above.

Candidates are reminded that if a pencil is used for diagrams/sketches it must be dark (HB or B).

Coloured pens, coloured pencils and highlighter pens must **not** be used.

Answer in the boxes on the next page.

Design idea 1

(8 marks)

Design idea 2

(8 marks)

Total: 16 marks

14 The picture shows a squeezy plastic bottle made from Low Density Polyethene (LDPE).

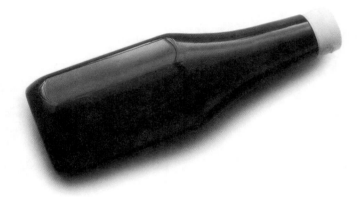

14 (a) Give two properties of polyethene that make it suitable for making the plastic bottle.

For each property, justify your answer.

Property 1:

....

....

(1 mark)

Justification:

....

....

(1 mark)

Property 2:

....

....

(1 mark)

Justification:

....

....

(1 mark)

14 (b) Polyethene is a thermoplastic.

Describe one characteristic of a thermoplastic.

Characteristic:

....

....

(2 marks)

14 (c) The environment is an important consideration for manufacturers in today's society.

Give two types of pollution that should be carefully controlled by the manufacturer of the squeezy plastic bottle.

Pollution 1:

....

....

(1 mark)

Pollution 2:

....

....

(1 mark)

14 (d) What process is used to make polythene bottles?

....

(2 marks)

14 (e) Describe why there is no waste when a polythene is made into bottles.

....

....

....

....

(2 marks)

Total 12 marks

Notes